METAIRIE, AMES, HIGH

METAIRIE, AMES, HIGH

The Streets of Jefferson Parish

EARL J. HIGGINS

PELICAN PUBLISHING COMPANY

Gretna 2011

*The word "Pelican" and the depiction of a pelican are trademarks
of Pelican Publishing Company, Inc., and are registered in the
U.S. Patent and Trademark Office.*

Library of Congress Cataloging-in-Publication Data

Higgins, Earl J.
  Metairie, Ames, High : the streets of Jefferson Parish / Earl J.
Higgins.
       p. cm.
  Includes index.
  ISBN 978-1-58980-887-4 (pbk. : alk. paper)
  1. Jefferson Parish (La.)—History, Local—Anecdotes. 2. Street
names—Louisiana—Jefferson Parish—History—Anecdotes.
3. Jefferson Parish—Biography—Anecdotes. I. Title.
  F377.J4H44 2011
  976.3'38—dc22

                                            2010042934

Printed in the United States of America

Published by Pelican Publishing Company, Inc.
1000 Burmaster Street, Gretna, Louisiana 70053

For Janet, who grew up on
Jefferson Avenue in Old Metairie

Contents

Introduction

In 1949, Jefferson Parish was just beginning its expansive growth following World War II. In that period of shared relief that the war was over and confidence in the future, an important book appeared in New Orleans. It was *Frenchmen, Desire, Good Children and Other Streets of New Orleans*. Written and illustrated by John Chase, the editorial cartoonist for the *New Orleans States*, then one of the city's afternoon newspapers, it used the streets of New Orleans as a matrix for presenting the rich and colorful history of the Crescent City. Lighthearted and easy to read, *Frenchmen* soon became a New Orleans classic, necessary reading for anyone wanting to understand the fascinating complexity of the city's history and geography. The book has gone through many printings, a second edition, and a change of publisher, and it remains a prominent fixture in the "local interest" sections of bookstores in south Louisiana.

Jefferson Parish is an outgrowth of New Orleans; its history and development are inextricably connected to the city, which was already more than one hundred years old before Jefferson Parish came into existence. As Jefferson Parish grew more urban in the nineteenth century, its east bank towns of Lafayette, Jefferson City, and Carrollton were absorbed by the city of New Orleans, becoming parts of the metropolis that was growing larger and wealthier. Until the middle of the twentieth century, Jefferson Parish was rural and agricultural. There were areas of it so remote and isolated that they could be reached only by water. Even at midcentury there were many of Jefferson's native-born

American citizens for whom English was a difficult language to speak and understand.

The evolution of Jefferson Parish from rural and remote to a modern American suburbia is a function of the automobile and the postwar economic expansion. As more and more families acquired automobiles, more and more streets were needed for them to drive on, streets on which new homes could be built to accommodate a population made more mobile by personally owned motor vehicles.

Hundreds of streets were built in Jefferson Parish during the postwar boom. Although the building of residential neighborhoods eventually slowed down, it continues in places in the parish where the available land is safeguarded, it is hoped, by hurricane-protection levees. Developments south of Marrero, on land once a dense forest, were built in the first decade of the twenty-first century, and the trend continues. Jefferson Parish on both sides of the Mississippi River is and will continue to be primarily a residential suburb to the city of New Orleans, a suburbia of motor vehicles and the streets on which they move.

Jefferson is more than that, of course, as is made evident by the shipyards and other marine industries and those facilities that support the oil and gas production in the Gulf of Mexico. Grand Isle and the communities of the Lafitte-Barataria region continue the centuries-old occupations of catching shrimp, crabs, fish, and oysters and processing them for commercial use.

The dependence on boats and railroads to move people and goods in and out of Jefferson Parish is no more. The streets, roads, and expressways are the principal bases of the transportation system, streets and roads that have been given names by their creators, just as parents choose names for their children. Where do all those names come from? Who gets to pick? How did a certain name get on a particular street? These are questions you might ask while driving around Jefferson Parish. Sometimes the answer is easy, the name of **Jefferson Highway** for example. Other names require some inquiry, some digging into history. Some street names are so obscure and from so long ago that learning the story behind them is virtually impossible. A developer may have wished to celebrate a member of the family or reward an investor in the project. The reasons for a street's name are usually not part of the official ordinance establishing the street or development. The parish council or the councils of the incorporated municipalities that approve the names of streets are usually satisfied for official purposes that the names are not offensive.

Unlike the city of New Orleans, Jefferson Parish has no single, central pattern of streets from which the political, social, economic, and personal histories of the city grew. There is no Metairie equivalent of the Vieux Carré. There is in Jefferson Parish no equivalent of Jackson Square or the magnificence of St. Louis Cathedral, the Presbytere, and the Cabildo and all the history and mystery associated with those structures and the streets of the French Quarter. There are, however, many neighborhoods, subdivisions, and housing developments with streets whose names give hints to the history and culture of the parish.

Although inspired by Chase's *Frenchmen, Desire, Good Children,* this book will cover more than the history of Jefferson Parish as seen through its streets. The history of the parish has been thoroughly covered in many books, many of which have been referenced in the writing of this more lighthearted study. There will be history discussed to be sure, but also geography, geology, etymology, and even a chapter based on dendrology—the study of trees. There will be examination of the origin of the names of some streets, the meanings of some of the names, and a few misspellings and other faux pas. Necessarily there are a lot of facts and what might be called trivia, which are often fun to know.

Actual street names, past and present, appear in **bold print.** For comparison or illustration, there are a few street names that are imaginary or fictional or never proceeded beyond a proposal. They will not appear in bold print.

Occasionally imbedded in the chapters are questions about Jefferson Parish and related matters to challenge the reader. There is no grade given for wrong or right answers, although readers might want to test their acumen. The answers will be reached after completing each chapter.

Drive, bicycle, or walk around, reading the street signs. There's a lot to learn and enjoy about the streets of Jefferson Parish.

METAIRIE, AMES, HIGH

Chapter 1

Tchoupitoulas Parish?

Jefferson. The name is instantly recognizable. Thomas Jefferson is one of the giants of history, someone inextricably interwoven with the concepts of self-determination, democracy, and America. At age thirty-three he drafted the Declaration of Independence of the United States, setting in motion political and social movements that changed the world. He was the third president of the United States, and during his presidency and against his political philosophy of limited government he authorized the purchase of the Louisiana Territory from France, more than doubling the size of the new nation by the act of sale. Jefferson was an inventor, a scientist, a lawyer, and a prolific man of letters. His visage appears on the infrequently used two-dollar bill and on the millions of five-cent coins. Few people have had as much influence on the course of history as has Thomas Jefferson. He died on July 4, 1826, exactly fifty years after the adoption of his Declaration of Independence by the thirteen states of the new United States.

Every state in the union has multiple place names honoring the great man. There are Jefferson counties, Jefferson schools, and creeks and streams named Jefferson. There is a Jefferson Street or Jefferson Avenue or Jefferson Road just about everywhere. The capital city of Missouri is named for him. Nobel Prize-winning author William Faulkner named the center of his fictional world of Yoknapatawpha County the town of Jefferson.

On February 11, 1825, about sixteen months before he died, the legislature of the State of Louisiana honored

Thomas Jefferson by naming a new parish for him. This new Jefferson Parish was immediately upriver from New Orleans, a city already more than one hundred years old and growing steadily in population and wealth. Like New Orleans, Jefferson Parish included both sides of the Mississippi River, even without a public ferry system. Bridges spanning the wide Mississippi were hardly a dream then, and the first one would not be built for more than another one hundred years. Jefferson became the second Louisiana parish named for a U.S. president, the first being, appropriately, Washington Parish in 1819. Jackson, Grant, and Lincoln parishes would follow many years later.

The name Jefferson, although familiar and popular, was not the only candidate for the appellation to be given to the new parish. Already for several generations the east bank of the Mississippi River above New Orleans, from where the Garden District is now located to where Colonial Country Club nestles against the levee in the city of Harahan, was called by Louisianians the "Tchoupitoulas Coast." The country club site was originally the Tchoupitoulas Plantation. The original Tchoupitoulas people, long before the arrival of Europeans and Africans, knew the value of waterfront property.

The spelling varied; sometimes it was "Chapatoulas," sometimes "Chapitoula," sometimes "Chapitulas." The name was derived from a dialect of the Choctaw language, and the general consensus is that it refers to "people who live along the river." Eventually the French spelling became the standard, a more or less phonetic interpretation because the native Indians had no written language, and that spelling continues today, "Tchoupitoulas." (The silent T also shows up in the spelling of another Choctaw-derived name of a river that flows into Lake Pontchartrain, Tchefuncte.)

Today the Tchoupitoulas Coast is covered with wharves from the Garden District upriver to Audubon Park, at which point some high-rise condominiums have towers above the levee overlooking where once were the homes of the humble batture dwellers, squatters on the land between the levee and the river. The batture dwellers have been evicted from the Orleans Parish side of the line, but Jefferson Parish has been more tolerant. The riverside dwellers are copycats of the Tchoupitoulas people who lived along the east bank when the Europeans first arrived. These batture dwellers are still there, a few of them, not owning the land on which their homes are built, not living on any street.

There was a movement in the early 1820s to name the new upriver parish Tchoupitoulas Parish. This was logical because the name was already in use. However, that term did not refer to the west bank of the river, already burgeoning with agriculture and commerce. Thomas Jefferson's prestige was growing as he became an elder statesman, and the English-speaking residents were increasing in number and political influence. Residents of Jefferson Parish today should be grateful to those who prevailed in getting the legislature to adopt the name Jefferson. It is much easier to spell, the name needs no explanation when spoken to outsiders, and it is better to be known as "Jeffersonians" than as "Tchoupitoulans" or "Tchoupitoulese." ("You live *where?*" "How do you spell that?" "What's that mean?" And so forth.)

There is much power in the opportunity to name something. The given name becomes associated with the place, and the perception of what occurs there and who lives there is generated by the mention of the name, a meaning reinforced by the passage of years. Once a place is named, it is usually difficult to change the name, especially if the general usage of the population prefers to keep the older name. In New Orleans, the Roosevelt Hotel was considered the *grande dame* of the hospitality, entertainment, and tourism industry. It was purchased in the 1970s by investors from elsewhere who changed the name to the Fairmont-Roosevelt then to just the Fairmont. Many in the New Orleans area ignored the name change and continued to refer to the hotel as the Roosevelt. The

building was severely damaged by flood waters from the
broken levees following Hurricane Katrina in 2005, and the
building was closed. New investors refurbished the structure
and restored it to its historic elegance. Just as important,
they restored the name "The Roosevelt" when it opened in
2009. A place name is important not just for identification
but for historical continuity and a sense of identity.

Naming is serious business. There are at least four
score and seven books, pamphlets, and Web sites to which
prospective parents can refer when picking a name for their
children. There are analyses of names, their ethnic origins,
their meanings, whether teachers will treat a student with
a particular name better or less favorably, and whether
certain names appeal to or repulse potential spouses and
employers. An international committee of meteorologists
meets every year to determine the names of the tropical
storms and hurricanes for the next season. They look over
their six-year list and make adjustments. The names of
storms that have caused much misery and destruction are
retired forever. Never again will Audrey or Betsy or Camille
or Katrina threaten Louisiana or any place else in North
America or the Caribbean. The selection of a name is not to
be taken lightly, whether for a hurricane, a child, a parish,
or a street.

Some streets become so identified with an industry that
many people lose track of the fact that they are specific
geographical locations. Say the name **Wall Street,** and
the image is not of a roadway in New York City filled with
vehicles and lined with tall buildings, but of the heart of
capitalism, the financial center of the world. The same
reference to industry rather than to place goes for the
name **Madison Avenue,** synonymous with the advertising
industry. The street name **Broadway** is not just a street; it
is the apex of the theater and drama industry.

It is a point of irony that Thomas Jefferson did not
think that places should be named for living persons. In
a letter of September 23, 1800, to his friend and frequent

correspondent Dr. Benjamin Rush, Jefferson expressed disapproval of the practice. He wrote: "Death alone can seal the title of any man to this honor by putting it out of his power to forfeit it." The Louisiana legislature was either unaware of or ignored Jefferson's opinion because he was still alive when Jefferson Parish came into existence.

Wise sage that he was, Thomas Jefferson had made a very good observation in his letter. If a person is still alive after being honored with a dedicated street or other place name, he has an indefinite period in which to remain revered, become more famous, or create embarrassment for those who named the street or place in his honor. Dictators and despots who have streets, airports, and other places named for themselves see the street signs change if their enforced popularity evaporates when they lose power or die. The city of St. Petersburg, Russia, became Leningrad in the Soviet Union, then Petrograd when Lenin was officially in disgrace, then back to St. Petersburg when the Soviet Union dissolved and just Russia remained. In St. Bernard Parish a major thoroughfare was named **Judge Perez Drive** in honor of the late Judge Leander H. Perez Sr., the arch-segregationist who was the political boss of St. Bernard and Plaquemines parishes in the 1950s and 1960s and who vigorously opposed the desegregation of any public facilities. As years passed it became something of an embarrassment that the major street of the parish was named for such an opponent of racial progress and harmony. But, serendipitously, there was another judge of the parish, popular and progressive, named Perez, Judge Melvin Perez. So the parish leaders decided that the official name **Judge Perez Drive** would honor the latter judge, acceptable to all citizens, and there was no need to change the street signs or for businesses to change the addresses on their letterheads. There have been changes in street names in Jefferson Parish, too, but nothing like the experience of **Judge Perez Drive**.

Even more than seventy-five years after his death, Huey P. Long remains a controversial figure in Louisiana history, but his accomplishments overrode his darker side. Jefferson Parish's only bridge across the Mississippi River keeps his name, as does one of the major streets of the parish's seat of government, Gretna, in **Huey P. Long Avenue.** Today people sometimes refer to the bridge as simply "the Huey" or "the Huey P." without thinking about the man for whom the span was named. And what about the lake and all the other places and streets named for a French official, Louis XIV's minister of marine, Count Pontchartrain? Kenner's **Rue Place Pontchartrain** is one of them. The historical reference and identification of the person named disappears into everyday usage of the name identifying the geographical location.

For most of its history, Jefferson Parish had few streets to which to give names. Jefferson was a rural, agricultural domain that was linear, following the higher land along both banks of the Mississippi River and the Metairie Ridge. There were many small farms and some larger plantations. Transportation of goods and people was done, whenever possible, by water. The roads and streets consisted of lanes of dirt full of ruts that became mud during rain. Most of the streets were on private land and had no names or were given names by the farmers or plantation owners. For example, **Christmas Road,** which is now part of the Barataria Preserve of the Jean Lafitte National Historical Park and Preserve, was named for the Christmas Plantation on which it was located in the latter part of the nineteenth century.

Unlike the adjacent city of New Orleans, which was laid out in a grand plan with a grid of streets named by the trio of John Law, the Scotsman who was Louisiana's first real-estate developer; Adrien de Pauger, Law's engineer who created the plan; and Jean-Baptiste Le Moyne, Sieur de Bienville, the French-Canadian first governor of the French colony of Louisiana and the founder of New Orleans, Jefferson Parish had no cohesive plan. It grew because of its proximity to New Orleans and the financial and export opportunities that city afforded. It was not until around the time of the founding of Jefferson Parish in 1825 that the era of the great plantations began.

The coming of the steamboat in the first part of the nineteenth century and the development of the process for the mass granulation of sugar in the 1790s on a plantation at what is now Audubon Park in New Orleans created a demand for more and more acreage of sugarcane. The steamboats could carry far more cargo than flatboats or boats propelled by sails and oars. The plantations of Jefferson Parish prospered during that period, but with the dark reality of wealth being produced by slave labor. The Mississippi River was the principal "street" on which commerce was carried. The road along the levee on the east bank was an upriver extension of **Tchoupitoulas Street** that began in New Orleans. The street was also known by the matter-of-fact name of **River Road,** a name that eventually stuck, probably in part because it was easier for English-only speakers to say and spell.

In its early years, Jefferson Parish included the east bank cities of Lafayette, Jefferson, and Carrollton, but the city of New Orleans annexed those municipalities one by one. After the absorption of those towns, Jefferson Parish remained largely rural and agricultural well into the twentieth century. Small dairies, vegetable and poultry farms, and horse-and-mule operations on both sides of the river supported a growing city of New Orleans with milk, meat, and produce. Because there were no urban areas, there was no need for a system of public streets.

Veteran newspaper columnist Hermann Deutsch, who had written for the *New Orleans Item,* the *New Orleans States-Item,* and the *Times-Picayune,* wrote a reminiscence in 1958 about Jefferson Parish in 1917. He remembered that there were only four roads in the parish, **Metairie Road, River Roads** along the levees on either side of the river, and an unnamed road from Marrero to Lafitte. (At least it was unnamed to Deutsch's knowledge.) None of these dirt roads was passable its entire length in wet weather, Deutsch wrote. In 1917 **Jefferson Highway** and **Airline Highway** had yet to be built.

Although by the 1920s there was a good bit of residential construction and the necessary streets to support those developments, the big boom in Jefferson Parish came after World War II when returning veterans, assisted by the G.I. Bill, which provided them with home financing, began constructing and buying homes by the thousands, a residential building boom that lasted more than twenty years. Hundreds of new streets were designed, graded, and named in the building expansion as Jefferson shifted from a rural society to a suburban community.

All those new streets needed names so that residents could explain where they lived and where the mail was to be sent. Now that he is dead, Thomas Jefferson should be flattered that Jefferson Parish was named for him, and he can smile upon the many streets in the parish that carry his name: **Jefferson Highway** across the east bank; **Jefferson Street, Jefferson Heights Avenue, and Jefferson Park Avenue** in Old Jefferson; **Jefferson Avenue** in Old Metairie; **Jefferson Street** in Gretna; and **Jefferson Avenue** on Grand Isle.

Chapter 2
Name that Street

What's in a name? That which we call a rose by any other name would smell as sweet.

Shakespeare put those words into the mouth of a love-sick Juliet, telling Romeo that it made no difference to her that he was a member of a family at war with hers. Juliet was wrong. Names carry a lot of meaning. They identify the person or place well beyond the simple, basic meaning of the name. New Orleans's **Bourbon Street,** for example, is synonymous with partying and raucous street behavior. Few if any revelers there contemplate the fact that the street was named for a royal family, not for whiskey made in Kentucky. If a real-estate developer or members of the Jefferson Parish Council want to convey the image of a residential development as pleasant, safe, and serene, they would not select "Bourbon" for a street name. There is no Bourbon Street in Jefferson. Nor are there Scotch, Vodka, Gin, or Tequila streets either.

A real-estate developer cannot proceed with a project creating a new residential subdivision without the approval of the Jefferson Parish Council for land in the unincorporated areas of the parish. In the incorporated towns and cities, the councils of those municipalities must give their respective authorizations. The process is in the form of ordinances. In addition to meeting the requirements of lot size, drainage, and placement of utilities, the developer must submit proposed names for the streets being created. The council can disapprove of names it decides are inappropriate. No developer in his right mind would propose, for example, to name streets after noxious people or substances. Who wants to buy a house on Hitler Avenue or invite guests to dinner on Arsenic Street? On the other hand, there is at least one Jefferson Parish street that violates this principle dramatically. In Marrero, a driver can turn off **Lapalco Boulevard** onto **Hurricane Path.** The word "hurricane" by itself causes anxiety and fear in any Jeffersonian who lived through Hurricane Betsy in 1965, Hurricanes Katrina and Rita in 2005, and Hurricanes Gustav and Ike in 2008. Further, calling the street a "path" for the hurricane to travel seems to be an invitation for the strongest storm on earth to come right into the heart of the parish. There's a reason for the scary name; the street is next to L. W. Higgins High School, and the school's mascot name is the Hurricanes. They're not trying to induce people to buy homes on that street. Nevertheless, there are apartments on **Hurricane Path.** It doesn't sound like a comforting, cozy place to live.

The developer can be cautious and conservative and give the planned streets sequentially numbered names: First, Second, Third, and so on. Such names, however, do not generally catch the attention of prospective buyers, and the message they convey is of generic sameness. It takes years, even generations, before a street with a number for a name becomes synonymous with elegance and style. The numbered street names of the Garden District of New Orleans became symbols of wealth and style long after fine homes were built there. Perhaps the most famous street with a number name is New York's **Fifth Avenue.** The name immediately makes one think of beautiful people, high fashion, and even higher prices. **Fifth Street** in Harvey does not and probably never will have the cachet associated with **Fifth Avenue** in New York.

There are streets with only numbers for names in many communities in Jefferson Parish. Kenner's **Third Street** is really a westward continuation of **Reverend Richard Wilson Drive** and **Jefferson Highway** from River Ridge, and it becomes **River Road** at the St. Charles Parish line. In the area of Metairie occasionally referred to as New Metairie, a series of east-west numbered streets begins near Lake Pontchartrain with **Third Street** and proceeds in orderly fashion south block by block until **Forty-Ninth Street** ends the series. Where are First and Second streets? It seems they disappeared under the Lake Pontchartrain levee as hurricane protection assumed greater emphasis long after the initial grid of streets was laid out.

Fourth Street on the Westbank was once the main street from Gretna west through Harvey, Marrero, and Westwego. Bridge City reveals its industrial and commercial origin at the end of the Huey P. Long Bridge with a no-nonsense pattern of numbered streets. They are crossed by streets named **Industry** and **Commerce**, and the main roadway through the community is **Bridge City Avenue.** No fancy names in this solid blue-collar neighborhood; what you see is what you get.

In the floods following Hurricane Katrina in 2005, the Seventeenth Street Canal, usually written as "17th Street," achieved international notoriety. It was one of the drainage canals whose levees gave way and flooded 80 percent of the city of New Orleans. The 17th Street Canal divides Orleans and Jefferson parishes, and Jefferson was spared when the levees on its side of the canal held, just barely. Across the canal, torrents of water nearly washed the Lakeview neighborhood away. However, if one checks a street map for 17th Street, there is no street by that name close to the canal. In Metairie, **Seventeenth Street** is one of the numbered east-west streets crossing **Causeway Boulevard.** The 17th Street Canal's namesake is gone. In 1894 the street's name in Orleans Parish was changed to **Palmetto Street.** At the parish line, however, the canal kept its old name, which now endures in post-Katrina infamy.

There once was a neighborhood of number-named streets in River Ridge. When the Upstream Subdivision was first laid out in the 1950s, the developer gave the streets

parallel to **Jefferson Highway** simple number names. There
were already such names in nearby Kenner, where they had
been so named for one hundred years. At first the streets
in Upstream were barely there. The surfaces were dirt or
clam and oyster shells; the drainage was through ditches
alongside the streets. After a few lots were sold and the
developers and landowners needed catchy names to attract
attention in the residential-building boom of the early
1960s, they decided that names of old plantation homes
would be more attractive to prospective buyers than just
numbers. They came up with both well-known and little-
known names to conjure up visions of the Old South. There
are **Rosedown Place** and **Ormond Place,** but also **Chretien
Point Place, Bocage Place, Darby Place,** and **Belle Cherie
Place.**

Rosedown is a popular tourist site near St. Francisville,
Louisiana; Ormond is on the east bank **River Road** in St.
Charles Parish. Chretien Point is north of Lafayette; Bocage
is also on the east bank **River Road** below Baton Rouge,
upriver from the **Sunshine Bridge.** Darby is the name of
two plantations, one in Georgia and one in South Carolina.
Belle Cherie is on Bayou Tortue in St. Martin Parish. None
of the streets in the Upstream Subdivision is named for a
Jefferson Parish plantation from days of old.

How do streets, such as those in the Upstream Subdivision, get their names changed? If, in comparison, someone
wants to change his personal name, that person must file
a petition in state court. The district attorney informs the
judge whether the name change will further anything illegal. If not, the judge usually signs an approval judgment
making the new name official. However, changing street
names is done in unincorporated Jefferson Parish by a petition to the parish council. The proponents present their
case, and the council members consider the reasons for the
change and any opposition. Then an ordinance is passed
officially changing the name. The process is similar in the
incorporated municipalities of the parish.

Not so if the street is a state highway. Only the Louisiana legislature can change the name of a state highway. For example, in 1999 civic leaders were trying to change the image of **Airline Highway**, along with its reputation for sleaze and commercial sex. They asked the legislature to soften the thoroughfare's name by calling it **Airline Drive**. As a result, the road that begins as **Airline Highway** in Orleans Parish at the end of **Tulane Avenue** extends for about a mile to the Jefferson Parish line, where it becomes **Airline Drive**. It remains a "drive" until it reaches westward to St. Charles Parish, at which point it becomes **Airline Highway** again, a name that it keeps until it ends in Baton Rouge.

Airline Drive has improved its image since the name change. In truth, the process began before the new name. Some—far from all—of the seedy bars and motels are gone, new retail outlets have opened, and Zephyr Field, home of the minor-league New Orleans Zephyrs baseball team, have made the name "drive" fit. Slowly, very slowly, **Airline Drive** is losing its identity as a street of lowlifes and hard-luck stories.

Getting the right names for the streets in a residential subdivision is very important for the developers. They want to pick names that are pleasing, names that will attract potential buyers in the income range sought for the lots and homes. Jefferson Parish has many subdivisions made up of streets with noncontroversial names. Somewhere in the real-estate developers' handbook there must be columns of names that can be combined to create compound names that can be used anywhere, whether in Jefferson Parish or in Jefferson City, Missouri.

One of the first rules of the handbook seems to be that a street is never called a "street." That's too prosaic. Something more elegant is needed to appeal to potential buyers. Here are a couple of hypothetical lists that a developer could use. The names of many Jefferson Parish streets created since the 1940s seem as though they were crafted from such lists. This process is similar to the way menus in

Chinese restaurants were once printed: Take one from column A and one from column B, combine them for dinner.

Column A		Column B	
Hill	Village	Crest	Dale
Oak (or the	Stone	Brook	Circle
name of	Mill	Gate	Lane
any tree)	Forest	Wood	Way
Glen	Park	Creek	
Meadow	Spring	Hollow	

The developer, using these lists, can come up with "Glen Brook" or "Glenbrook" for one street, "Stone Circle" for another, then mix them up and name two more streets "Glen Circle" and "Stone Brook." It's easy.

Avenue, Court, Place, and Road are available, too. Street almost never. One can envision a committee of developers opening the board for a game of Monopoly, not to test their investment instincts, but to see if they can come up with names that are as bland but as catchy as Park Place and New York Avenue.

Using an old-fashioned word to name a street sometimes adds charm to the neighborhood, even if the people who live on the streets are not completely sure what the archaic word means. An example of this practice is a group of streets in Harvey near Woodmere Park. The streets' names all end in "mere." There are **North** and **South Woodmere streets, Woodmere Court, Pointmere Drive, Oakmere Drive, Eastmere Street,** and **Westmere Street.** The "mere" is not a mere surplus ending, added to the main part of the name merely to make it sound better. Rather, "mere" is a term of an old British dialect meaning "a boundary or a boundary mark." Adding it to the basic word of the name makes the neighborhood sound more serene and posh.

There is always a risk in naming a street something that is not bland and noncontroversial. A perfectly respectable name may come to mean something unpleasant, disgusting, or insulting years later. For example, when **Manson Avenue** in Metairie was named, Charles Manson and his cult of killers had not yet made gory news by going on a murder spree. In Old Metairie **Fagot Avenue,** named for a prominent citizen of the early twentieth century, gets pronounced like the pejorative slang word for a male homosexual. Nevertheless, there probably have been no studies and surveys undertaken to see if the names of **Manson Avenue** and **Fagot Avenue** have had any lowering effect on the property values and sale prices of the homes on those streets.

Chapter 3
Honoring the Warriors

The creation of Jefferson Parish as a residential suburb of New Orleans began in earnest following World War II. In 1944 Congress passed legislation giving huge financial benefits to returning service men and women. Known as the G.I. Bill, the legislation provided money to educate people who would never have gone to college and loans to people who could never have afforded to buy homes. These benefits, the "thanks of a grateful nation," prevented a postwar recession and created an expansive middle class that generated wealth and made the United States the richest nation in the world. Jefferson Parish was part of that success.

Veterans came home from the war full of optimism and confidence. Unlike other belligerents in World War II, the United States entered peacetime virtually unscathed, and it had new factories and infrastructures built for the war efforts. The enemies of freedom had been soundly defeated, and millions of Americans had participated in the war, in and out of uniform. There was much pride in accomplishment and vigorous belief in a prosperous future.

As residential developments spread rapidly across Jefferson Parish in the late 1940s and 1950s, there was a general consensus to honor those who had served in the armed forces and contributed to the great victory. A public display of that honor was manifested in naming streets after heroes of the war and for all veterans in general. Single monuments are fine, but they may be missed or simply ignored by people driving past. Streets, on the other hand, have signs with names at every corner, read daily by many, reminding them of the person or groups of people honored in the name of the roadway. There were many new streets to name in postwar Jefferson Parish, and those streets were places for veterans and their families to display the new prosperity in their homes that were being furnished with black-and-white television sets, freezers, and TV dinners. They could drive dual- and triple-colored chrome-and-fins automobiles along roads with pleasant, comfortable, triumphant names that were not streets but mostly avenues, lanes, places, courts, and parkways.

One of the first projects to remember World War II veterans started in the New Jersey State Council of Garden Clubs in 1944. They planted flowers and shrubs along roadways to honor serving members of the armed forces. The name "Blue Star" came from the organization the Blue Star Mothers of America, for those who had a family member in the armed services and were eligible to fly a flag with a blue star from their homes. The idea caught on with garden clubs around the country, and memorial plaques were erected along highways and streets with a big blue star embossed, designating the roadway a Blue Star Memorial Highway to pay tribute to members of the armed forces. The practice spread to garden clubs throughout the country. Eventually in Jefferson Parish there were markers on **Jefferson Highway;** at the Moisant Airport, which would later be named New Orleans International Airport and even later Louis Armstrong International Airport; at the foot of the **Huey P. Long Bridge** on the Westbank; and at Lafreniere Park. There was no system of upkeep and repair of the memorial markers, and several were damaged and removed. The destructive swath of Hurricane Katrina included the marker on **Jefferson Highway.** Nevertheless, the war heroes had not been forgotten as other streets were dedicated to them.

The broad roadway known today as **Veterans Memorial Boulevard** is the main street of Metairie, the east Jefferson

commercial thoroughfare that took over that status from
Metairie Road and **Airline Highway.** In the early days of its
existence in the 1950s, **Veterans Memorial Highway** was
a street growing west, some of it not even paved, gleaming
bright white in the sunlight reflected off the clam and oyster
shells used as its roadbed. **Veterans Memorial Highway**
soon became known by its short name of simply **"Vets,"** a
one-syllable word that did well in television commercials as
the highway became the center of automobile dealerships
that provided new and used cars to the growing population of
Jefferson Parish.

But **Veterans Memorial Highway** was ugly. There
were generous regulations or lack thereof for commercial
development on both sides of the huge canal that separated
the four-lane roadway. The canal was often a place to throw
trash, for weeds to grow, and for stench to be generated. This
was no way to honor the war heroes to whom the street had
been dedicated. Eventually the canal was covered along several
blocks of its length, beginning at the Orleans Parish line to
Hessmer Avenue. Grass, trees, and shrubs were planted, and
the results of the efforts resembled a park. Later, other sections
of **Vets** were covered and landscaped, and large modern
sculptures were erected. More care was given to keeping the
grass on the canal banks cut. The bald cypress trees grew
rapidly and stately. The name of the street was changed
to **Veterans Memorial Boulevard** to make it sound more
elegant and to make a break with the past. The new streets
signs eliminated the "Memorial" part of the name, stating
only **"Veterans Boulevard."** The "Memorial" was surplus
anyway. A street named "Veterans" must necessarily be
dedicated to remembering all those who have served in
uniform, not just to honor veterans of a particular war. A
large memorial was erected to all veterans at the boulevard's
intersection with **Causeway Boulevard,** a fitting homage to
the warriors. The canal is still home to waterfowl, turtles,
and an occasional nutria, but the seediness of the past has
been generally controlled.

Other streets in Jefferson Parish are named for specific war heroes. **MacArthur Avenue** in Harvey remembers General of the Army Douglas MacArthur, the flamboyant, grandiose leader of allied forces in the southwest Pacific theater during World War II. He is best remembered for his promise to the people of the Philippines that, "I shall return," after retreating from the Japanese invasion early in the war. When he did return in 1944, he did so with great flair, with photographers taking pictures of him wading ashore from a landing craft, then solemnly announcing, "I have returned." During the Korean War a few years later, MacArthur was the leader of one of the most brilliant amphibious operations in history, the landing at Inchon, Korea, behind the enemy's main positions.

There is an **Eisenhower Street** in the Airline Park section of Metairie named for Dwight D. Eisenhower, General of the Army and later president of the United States from 1953 to 1961. As supreme commander of allied forces in Europe in World War II, Eisenhower was in charge of the 1944 invasion of Normandy and the liberation of Western Europe.

Whoever named a group of streets in Harahan must have been a veteran or veterans of the war in the Pacific during World War II. There are **Nimitz Drive, Halsey Drive, McArthur Drive,** and **Wainwright Drive,** which are evidence that the streets were named after World War II during the rapid expansion of residential neighborhoods. This section is located across **Jefferson Highway** from the Colonial Country Club. Fleet Admiral Chester W. Nimitz was the commander of U.S. Pacific forces in the central Pacific. Admiral William F. "Bull" Halsey was an aggressive commander of aircraft carrier task forces. The "McArthur" for whom the street is named is Douglas MacArthur, but the misspelling of his name on the Harahan street does not diminish his reputation as a great warrior—or as a great ego. General Jonathan Wainwright was the commander of American and Filipino forces surrounded by the invading Japanese on the Bataan Peninsula in the early days of World

War II. He led the doomed garrison with great bravery and
determination as the Japanese siege became more intense.
He held on for months, retreating to the old Spanish fortress
of Corregidor, where he eventually surrendered on May 6,
1942. Taken prisoner along with hundreds of his soldiers,
he endured the infamous Bataan Death March during which
hundreds died of starvation and mistreatment. Wainwright
survived and was liberated in August 1945. He was awarded
the Medal of Honor for his valor.

In addition to the heroes of the Pacific war, Harahan
honors General of the Army George C. Marshall with
Marshall Drive. General Marshall was the chief of staff of the
U.S. Army from 1939 until after the end of World War II in
1945. He was the head of the largest army in history, more
than eight million soldiers. He became secretary of state in
1947 and, while in that post, proposed what became known
as the Marshall Plan for rebuilding war-ravaged Europe.
Harahan also pays homage to the members of the Veterans
of Foreign War organization with **VFW Avenue.**

In Metairie, there are **Soldier Street, Army Street,** and
Navy Street. Did someone leave out the air force and the
Marines, or did they run out of streets to name at the time?
There is a **Marine Street** in Marrero, but its connection, if
any, to the U.S. Marine Corps is unclear. Near **Army, Navy,**
and Soldier streets are **Argonne Street** and **Meuse Street,**
named for the Argonne Forest and the Meuse River in
France where a huge battle was fought at the end of World
War I.

The U.S. Coast Guard does not usually think of itself as
a band of warriors, but they have been called upon and
performed admirably in most U.S. wars. The "Coasties"
are best known for their mission of and dedication to
marine safety and search and rescue. The Coast Guard's
spectacular performance in the aftermath of Hurricane
Katrina, rescuing thousands from the floodwaters caused
by the broken levees, was seen on live television around the
world. In Jefferson Parish, the Coast Guard has facilities

at opposite geographical ends. The Coast Guard Station at Bucktown in the northeast corner of the parish provides a base for overseeing and enforcing marine safety on Lake Pontchartrain and connecting waters. On the east end of Grand Isle, the southeast corner of the parish, is another Coast Guard station for service in the Gulf of Mexico, just outside the windows of the station. The Grand Isle Station was the site of a visit by President Barack Obama in 2010 for a briefing by Coast Guard Admiral Thad Allen to the governors of Louisiana, Mississippi, Alabama, and Florida, along with senators, mayors, and other elected officials concerning the crude oil gushing into the Gulf of Mexico from a broken drill pipe. To reach the Grand Isle Station, a traveler drives along **Admiral Craik Drive,** which is the most southeastern street in the parish. Other Jefferson streets named for generals and admirals state only their names; **Admiral Craik Drive** also gives the man's rank. Rear Admiral James D. Craik was the commandant of the Eighth Coast Guard District with headquarters in New Orleans and jurisdiction over a vast area including Jefferson Parish. During his tour of duty, the Coast Guard station on Grand Isle was constructed. He retired from the Coast Guard in 1966 and became the superintendent of the Texas Maritime Academy at Texas A & M University in Galveston.

Admiral Craik Drive is also the address of the Grand Isle State Park on the seaward side and Pirates Cove Marina and condominiums on the other. Here is an ironic situation: On the street named for an admiral of a federal organization with responsibility for maritime law enforcement there is an upscale vacation development named for maritime criminals. If someone asked where the Grand Isle Coast Guard Station is located, the correct answer is, "Right next door to the place named for pirates."

The invasion of Europe by allied forces on June 6, 1944, is the greatest amphibious assault in history. Before then the name Normandy designated only a region of northern France, the place from which an invading army crossed the English Channel in the opposite direction in 1066 and changed British history. After June 4, 1944, "Normandy" acquired a new meaning, a sense of combat and heroism, determination and death. Many Americans died in the invasion and the subsequent liberation of Europe; many more were maimed and wounded. Their sacrifices are remembered in streets named Normandy in Jefferson Parish. There is **Normandy Avenue** in Harahan, **Normandy Court** in the Estelle community south of Marrero, **Normandy Drive** in Kenner, and **Normandy Street** in Nine Mile Point. The street in Kenner is named for the region of France rather than the invasion of 1944 as is evident from its presence in a cluster of streets named for regions of France including **Brittany Drive** and **Anjou Drive**. The same can be said for **Normandy Court** in Estelle. Connected to it are two streets named for adjoining regions in France, **Alsace Court** and **Lorraine Court;** a block away is **Bretagne Court,** the region of France known in English as Brittany. Nevertheless, for most Americans, the name "Normandy" means the great battle of the Second World War. Also in Nine Mile Point is a street named **Utah Beach Drive.** Utah beach was the code name of one of the five landing zones on the coast of Normandy on June 6, 1944, a place where the American forces landed in addition to the better-known Omaha Beach. The person giving the name to this street must have had an identification with Utah Beach, perhaps as a participant, perhaps as a relative of a soldier who went ashore there.

Not far from **Utah Beach Drive** near Westwego is the Claiborne Gardens subdivision, with streets named for World War II generals. **Patton Lane** gets its name from the man who is probably the best-known American soldier of World War II, General George S. Patton Jr. He was portrayed by actor George C. Scott in the film *Patton.* General Joseph "Vinegar Joe" Stilwell was a brilliant eccentric, a linguist, and a passionate leader of U.S. and Chinese forces fighting in Burma. His name is on **Stillwell Lane,** with an extra *L* to add to the misspelled street names in Jefferson Parish.

The leader of the difficult fighting to oust the Germans from Italy was General Mark Clark, who is remembered in the subdivision by **North Clark Lane** and **East Clark Lane**. The sobriquet the "Unsung Hero of the Pacific War" is given to little-known General Walter Krueger, one of flamboyant General Douglas MacArthur's subordinates and a very effective operational commander. Whoever named **West Krueger Lane** and **East Krueger Lane** must have had great admiration for this soldier.

The only highway of the Interstate Highway system that crosses Jefferson Parish is **Interstate 10,** better known as I-10. It has no dedicated name. Some portions of the Interstate system elsewhere have been dedicated to important people or events. For example, **Interstate 10** from Slidell, Louisiana, east to exit 13 in southwestern Mississippi is the **Stephen E. Ambrose Memorial Highway,** in memory of the famous historian who lived out his last days in Bay St. Louis, Mississippi. He chronicled the American soldiers of World War II and was one of the founders of the National World War II Museum in New Orleans. Here's a question for the reader: Can anyone recall the names of any of Professor Ambrose's books?

Interstate 12, which runs in its entirety through the Florida parishes north of Lake Pontchartrain is officially dedicated as the **Republic of West Florida Parkway,** to provide a memorial to remember one of the more obscure events in Louisiana's history. In September 1810, the Anglo inhabitants of Spanish West Florida declared themselves to be independent from Spain, which officially but only nominally had control over that region. The area was east of the Mississippi River, north of Lake Pontchartrain and Bayou Manchac, south of the thirty-first parallel of latitude, and east of the Pearl River. The republic lasted for seventy-four days, and then the region was incorporated into the United States and the territory of Orleans. It became known as the Florida Parishes, a name that continues today.

Jefferson Parish has no such names or colorful history

for its section of **I-10.** But the entire national Interstate system is named for Dwight D. Eisenhower, who proposed it and began constructing it while he was president. As an army officer in World War I, Eisenhower had accompanied a convoy of trucks across the continent from the Atlantic to the Pacific. There was no federal system of roads then, and the trip took two months. He saw the need for a federal road system to support national defense policies. Eisenhower had also studied the German transportation system, and he was impressed at the efficiency and speed of the movement of men and military materials along that system. The initial idea of Eisenhower's interstate highway system was to provide a linked and sturdy road system over which military convoys could traverse the country. The use of that system by private civilian vehicles was lagniappe, so to speak, because that wasn't the primary purpose of the highways.

General and President Eisenhower was one of America's greatest military leaders. As drivers proceed along the safe and smooth interstate highways, they would do well to remember Eisenhower's campaign slogan when he ran for president: "I like Ike."

Trivia answer: Professor Ambrose's titles include *Band of Brothers, Lewis and Clark: Voyage of Discovery,* and many more.

Chapter 4
Gretna

To enter Westbank Jefferson Parish from downtown New Orleans, a driver crosses the Mississippi River on the bridge called the **Crescent City Connection.** The first span of the bridge opened in 1958 and was given the plain vanilla name of **Greater New Orleans Bridge.** Thirty years later, after a second span was built, there was a contest in 1989 to give the double-span bridge a distinctive name. The contest was won by a Jefferson Parish student from St. Clement of Rome School in Metairie, Jennifer Grodsky. The name was later officially adopted by the state legislature.

The bridge does not reach Jefferson Parish, its Westbank end being in the Algiers section of New Orleans, but the city of Gretna can be entered from the first exit westbound. The **General DeGaulle Drive** exit branches into east and west. **General DeGaulle Drive** east becomes **Burmaster Street** when the roadway crosses the parish line into Jefferson Parish. **Burmaster Street,** named for a family that has been prominent in business and civic affairs in Gretna for several generations, extends toward the Mississippi River. Wendell Burmaster was one of the founders in 1935 and later the president of the Krewe of Choctaw, which originally began as a social club before starting a Mardi Gras parade. **Burmaster Street** crosses **Hancock Street,** named for John Hancock, whose distinctive signature on the Declaration of Independence is now used to sell life insurance. **Burmaster Street** also crosses **Franklin Avenue,** named for one of the wisest men in American history, Benjamin Franklin. He was an inventor, statesman, writer of *Poor Richard's Almanac,* and experimenter, investigating electricity by flying a kite in a thunderstorm.

This section of Gretna is called McDonoghville, its original name before Gretna came to be, the site of a plantation owned by John McDonogh, the famous philanthropist who gave his money to found the public-school systems of New Orleans and Baltimore. McDonogh was unusual for his time in that he allowed his slaves to work off their bondage and earn their freedom. Around the plantation there grew a community of freed slaves called Freetown, which later became McDonoghville. He is remembered and honored for his largesse in many ways, including a street by that name in the McDonoghville section of Gretna. Although John McDonogh spelled his name without a *u*, it gets spelled "McDonough" rather than **McDonogh Street** on maps both printed and electronic. McDonoghville's public school, McDonogh No. 26, honors his legacy. When the town of Gretna was incorporated in August 1913, it included McDonoghville and the adjacent village of Mechanikham, a settlement of German immigrants and their descendents.

The city's name is invoked by the prominent street called **Gretna Boulevard**, which extends beyond the city limits into the adjoining community of Harvey. Gretna gets its name from a place in Scotland, Gretna Green. The Scottish town was famous for "quickie" weddings; a judge there waived any waiting period and other administrative requirements, and eager couples in Scotland and England went to Gretna Green for quick and easy marriage ceremonies. It is still a marriage-destination town today, much like Niagara Falls or Las Vegas, but without the Elvis impersonators. A justice of the peace began the practice in Jefferson Parish, and the nearby neighborhood became associated with the town in Scotland and started to be called Gretna. The "Green" part of the name was quickly dropped, although not as quick as the weddings.

Gretna's first mayor was John Ehret, and his family remains involved in the civic and social affairs of the

Westbank. There is a street named for him, **Ehret Road**, but it is in Marrero, not Gretna.

In the early twentieth century, Gretna was sometimes called—or called itself—the "Brooklyn of the South." The Brooklyn Bridge over the East River in New York linked Manhattan with Brooklyn and helped that borough thrive. The people of Gretna (Gretnarians? Gretnish? Gretnese? Gretnoids?) longed for a bridge that would connect them to the big city of New Orleans. That dream and plan did not happen until the bridge from downtown New Orleans to Algiers was opened in 1958. There was no street named Brooklyn in Gretna, but there was a place referred to as the "Old Brooklyn Pasture," which became a residential development. There is a **Brooklyn Avenue** in adjacent Algiers in Orleans Parish—Algiers was sometimes referred to as the "Brooklyn of the South," too—but the street's name changes to **Madison Street** when it crosses into Jefferson Parish and Gretna. In nearby Harvey there is a **Brooklyn Avenue** as well as across the river in the Southport section of Old Jefferson. There, **Brooklyn Avenue** runs from **River Road** north past **Jefferson Highway** to the railroad tracks.

Whoever named a series of streets in Gretna had admiration for some of the great scientists and thinkers of history. Streets with the names **Kepler, Lavoisier, Newton,** and **Hero** show that the people naming them had an appreciation for science and that these streets were named before the trend of giving streets names that would help sell real estate. The same goes for Gretna streets **Virgil, Solon, Magellan,** and **Milton.**

Kepler Street remembers Johannes Kepler, a mathematician and astronomer who lived from 1571 to 1630 and developed the three laws of planetary motion. Antoine Lavoisier, an eighteenth-century French chemist, is considered the father of modern chemistry. Isaac Newton, British mathematician and physicist, is considered by most scientists to be the inventor of modern physics. Hero of Alexandria, an engineer, mathematician, and scientist in the ancient Greek world, invented the steam engine in the first century AD. However, it was not until the eighteenth century before it could be applied practically.

Contemporary street namers do not have the same appreciation for more recent scientists. There is no Einstein Street in Gretna or anywhere else in Jefferson Parish, even though Albert Einstein was without a doubt the most famous scientist of the twentieth century. Look in vain for streets named after Max Planck, the physicist who developed quantum mechanics, or physicist Robert Oppenheimer, considered the father of the atomic bomb. Any developer who wanted to name a street after Charles Darwin may run into opposition from religious fundamentalists, although there is a **Darwin Court** in Slidell, Louisiana. British mathematician and theoretical physicist Stephen Hawking produced a best-selling book about modern cosmology, *A Brief History of Time*. There is a **Hawkins Street** in Gretna but no Hawking Street. Scientists are not revered as they once were; here's a tough question for readers: Who can name a scientist who was a Nobel laureate in the past ten years?

Virgil is the renowned poet of ancient Rome, Publius Vergilius Maro, best known for his epic poem about the founding of Rome by refugees fleeing the destruction of ancient Troy, *The Aeneid*. Solon was a lawmaker in ancient Greece who vigorously supported the rule of law over the whims of rulers and others in power. Ferdinand Magellan was the Portuguese explorer who led the first trip around the world from 1519 to 1522. Magellan didn't make it all the way; he was killed in a battle on an island that would become the Philippines. Only one of his five ships made it back home. John Milton was the great English poet of the seventeenth century, best known for his epic work *Paradise Lost.*

Huey P. Long Avenue was originally named **Copernicus Street,** honoring the mathematician and astronomer who died in 1543. Nicholaus Copernicus's observations of the heavens led him to propose that, contrary to contemporary belief, the earth was not the center of the universe. Copernicus's theory caused a ruckus in academic and religious circles.

The name **Stumpf Boulevard** is not a misspelling of the word for what's left after a tree is cut down. This wide street traversing much of Gretna is named for John Stumpf and his family. John Stumpf, a physician and pharmacist, was active in commercial and civic affairs in Jefferson Parish. He was the founder and proprietor of a Gretna business called Stumpf's Magic Hoodoo Products. No, he did not sell gris-gris or other potions that might have been useful to the likes of Voodoo queen Marie Laveau; rather, he was in the business of sanitary supplies and insecticides. His advertisement proudly proclaimed that the Magic Hoodoo Products had won a World's Medal at the Panama-Pacific International Exposition in 1940. His Magic Hoodoo Products didn't need any gris-gris to be effective in killing bugs because his formula was based on a substance even more powerful, arsenic. John Stumpf's son Alvin, a pharmacist like his father, took over the business and also served for many years as a state senator representing Gretna. The Magic Hoodoo Products are no more, but descendants of John Stumpf are still involved in the life of Gretna and Jefferson Parish.

By far the largest and most traveled street in Gretna and on the Westbank is the **Westbank Expressway,** a street with no name beyond its location and function. A driver from New Orleans crossing the **Crescent City Connection** connects into the expressway simply by staying in the middle of the road. The expressway began in the 1950s as plans for the long-sought Mississippi River bridge were becoming a reality. Everyone knew that a bridge would make Gretna and the entire Westbank thrive. Before the expressway, traffic moving along the Westbank went through **Fourth** and **Fifth streets,** becoming more congested as more automobiles contributed to the post-World War II expansion. The first edition of the expressway was designed to move the east-west traffic away from the older sections of the Westbank to the south, where there was room for more commercial and residential development.

The first **Westbank Expressway** wasn't. There was nothing express about it. Although it was a divided, four-lane road, there were frequent traffic lights to prevent the traffic from being express. Eventually the elevated roadway made the expressway an authentic limited-access highway from the end of the Crescent City Connection past **Ames Boulevard** in Marrero. At that point the expressway ceases to be a limited-access roadway westward to its end at **Highway 90.**

The Jefferson Parish Council passed a resolution in October 2007 to ask the state legislature to rename the **Westbank Expressway** the **Harry Lee Expressway,** to honor Sheriff Harry Lee who had recently died. Sheriff Lee was probably the most popular politician in the history of Jefferson Parish, having served more than twenty years as sheriff. The legislature approved the name change for the elevated portion of the expressway only. The change went into effect in the summer of 2010 when signs were erected on the elevated roadway. The ground-level roadway parallel to the elevated expressway retains the name **Westbank Expressway** despite traffic lights every few blocks along its entire length.

Tucked between Algiers and Gretna is an unincorporated neighborhood called Terrytown. Terrytown is representative of the later stage of the postwar residential building boom of Jefferson Parish. The opening of the bridge across the Mississippi River in 1958 made the Westbank ripe for building bedroom communities for commuters to New Orleans and the east bank. Developer Paul Kapelow saw the opportunities, and he created a residential neighborhood right at the end of the new bridge. Terrytown was founded in March 1960. Kapelow was obviously a devoted family man because he named the development for his daughter

Terry and gave her name to the main street, **Terry Parkway,** which runs from the **Westbank Expressway** to **Belle Chasse Highway.** Kapelow honored his other daughter by naming the principal cross street of Terrytown **Carol Sue Avenue.**

Long before Terrytown was built, **Belle Chasse Highway** had been named for the plantation of someone who liked to hunt. The name "Belle Chasse" means "good hunting" in French. The "someone" was Judah P. Benjamin, a prominent New Orleans lawyer before the Civil War. Benjamin owned a plantation downriver from Jefferson Parish that he called Belle Chasse. He sold the plantation in 1850 and was elected U.S. senator from Louisiana in 1852. After the secession of the Confederacy, Benjamin became the attorney general of the Confederate States and later the secretary of war and the secretary of state. The community of Belle Chasse in Plaquemines Parish and **Belle Chasse Highway** are named for Benjamin's plantation.

At the eastern edge of Gretna and extending into adjacent Terrytown is a street named for booze, **Aquavit Street.** Aquavit is a brandylike spirit distilled from alcohol made from grain or potatoes and flavored with caraway seeds. It is a popular drink in Scandinavian countries. The street's name stands alone because there are no similarly named streets in the vicinity. It is parallel to and one block away from **Stumpf Boulevard,** and the nearby streets are named for people, flowers, or trees. The neighborhood would be more interesting if, along with **Aquavit,** there were streets named Kahlua, Grand Marnier, Chartreuse, and Benedictine.

Gretna is an incorporated city, the seat of government of Jefferson Parish. Do readers know the names of the other incorporated cities and towns of Jefferson Parish?

Trivia answers: Here are a few Nobel Prize-winning scientists: 2009—Ada E. Yonath in chemistry and Willard Boyle in physics; 2008—Harald zur Hausen in medicine and Yoichiro Nambu in physics. (They are not exactly household names, are they?)

The other incorporated municipalities of Jefferson Parish are the cities of Kenner, Harahan, and Westwego and the towns of Jean Lafitte and Grand Isle.

Chapter 5

¿Parlez-vous Italiano, Señorita?

Why is a Jefferson Parish street called a "rue" instead of a "street? Giving a street a name in a language other than English is a gimmick to draw the attention of prospective buyers to the street and to imbue it with elegance and class. Foreign names, especially French ones, give a certain cachet to the neighborhood and create a hope that the names will help improve property values. Sometimes a foreign name emphasizes some important historic event. Using foreign names for streets is also a function of contemporary popular culture, such as the trend to give newborn children Irish-, French-, Spanish-, or African-sounding names. Trends come and go in the names of children and streets, too.

Many streets in Jefferson Parish have names in languages other than English. Some of them are given names of people, places, or groups of people, such as **Chickasaw Street** in Metairie or **Segnette Boulevard** in Westwego. **West Esplanade Avenue** in Metairie is a French word that in English means, well, "esplanade," a wide street, obviously copied from **Esplanade Avenue** in New Orleans. (The name "**Esplanade Avenue**" is a bit of a redundancy; both words mean a "broad street.")

The Rio Vista neighborhood in Old Jefferson was developed in the 1920s, when all things Spanish were in vogue. Hundreds if not thousands of homes and some businesses in Orleans and Jefferson parishes were built during that period in a stucco-and-gallery design inspired by Spanish architecture. The trend shows up in the street names as well. **Rio Vista Avenue** means "river view," but the designers of that period thought it sounded better in Spanish. In that neighborhood there are streets named for saints, but in Spanish rather than English. **Santa Rosa Avenue, San Jose Avenue, San Carlos Avenue, San Mateo Avenue, and Santa Ana Avenue** crisscross the northern section of Rio Vista. These names reveal not only that the streets namer was interested in Spanish names and saints' names, but that the names of the saints are also geographical places in California, a state full of Spanish place names.

Santa Rosa is a city about fifty miles north of San Francisco. San Carlos and San Mateo are cities on the peninsula south of San Francisco. San Jose is the large city at the southern end of San Francisco Bay. **Santa Ana Avenue** is named for the city of Santa Ana in southern California—and also the name of the wildfire-driving winds common in the area. Fortunately, no Santa Ana winds blow on **Santa Ana Avenue** or elsewhere in Rio Vista. *Gracias a dios.*

Loma Linda Avenue on Grand Isle is Spanish for "beautiful hill." The street must be named for the city of that name in southern California because the only thing on Grand Isle that looks vaguely like a hill is the levee along the beach.

You can probably find a friend on **Amigo Street** in Estelle, but become sorrowful when turning onto nearby **Dolores Drive**. There is also a **Dolores Avenue** in Old Metairie as well as a **Dolores Drive** in the Live Oak Manor subdivision of Waggaman. It is obvious that these streets are not named to bring sorrow to those who live on them, but for ladies named Dolores.

In north Kenner there are *beaucoup* streets whose names begin with "chateau," the French word for a castle or manor house. In fact, the whole subdivision is called Chateau Estates and was designed to appeal to higher-end home buyers. There are **Chateau Magdelaine Drive, Chateau Haut Brion Drive,** and **Chateau Ausonne Drive,** among others named for wine-producing places in France.

One of Jefferson Parish's oldest and best-known streets also has a French name, **Metairie Road.** *Metairie* is an old French word for a farm on which the farmer splits the crop with the landowner, what in English might be called sharecropping. The word also conveys the sense of "small farm." Very early in the expansion of New Orleans, landowners were acquiring the higher land along the bayou and ridge they called Metairie for a place for growing food for growing New Orleans. It is ironic that Metairie and **Metairie Road** came to signify elegance and fine living from a word meaning a very humble farm.

In Marrero, **Kismet Street** and nearby **Deutsch Road** both intersect with **Barataria Boulevard.** In Turkish, Persian, and Arabic, "kismet" means "fate" or "destiny." There was once a Broadway musical production by that name. Perhaps the person who named the street liked the stage production rather than the actual meaning of the word. *Deutsch* is the German word for "German," although it is also a family name. By comparison, Bayou des Allemands and the town of Des Allemands in St. Charles Parish mean "Bayou of the Germans" in French.

There is a subsequent chapter about the name "Barataria," which comes from the Provençal language of the south of France and gives its name to **Barataria Boulevard.** Its basic meaning is "fraud" or "deceit."

There are many bayous in Louisiana, and there are several streets in Jefferson Parish with the word "bayou" in their names. South of the Estelle community of Marrero is a residential development called Bayou Estates. The streets in that subdivision are all named for Louisiana bayous, including **Bayou Boeuf, Bayou Teche,** and **Bayou Bleu drives,** among others. At the rear of the subdivision is a vestigial remnant of Bayou des Familles, once a distributary channel of the Mississippi River. The back street of the development is **Bayou des Familles Drive.** "Bayou" is an adaptation in French of *bayuk,* the Choctaw word for "stream." *Bayou des Familles* means "Bayou of

the Families," named in French for the families of Spanish
people from the Canary Islands who were settled along that
bayou by the Spanish colonial government in the eighteenth
century. Thus, in one name are Choctaw and French words
describing Spanish-speaking immigrants.

The first street inside Jefferson Parish on the east
bank, running from the **River Road** and crossing Jefferson
Highway is **Monticello Avenue.** At Jefferson Highway
the street continues on the opposite side of the roadway
but also on the opposite side of the protection levee, in
Orleans Parish. The protection levee is appropriate to the
name of the street, which is right up against the levee on
the upstream side in Jefferson and on the downstream
side in Orleans. In Italian, *monticello* means "little
mountain." The protection levee, much smaller than the
massive Mississippi River levee to which it connects, is a
manmade "little mountain." The name "Monticello" is best
known, however, as that of Thomas Jefferson's magnificent
and elaborate home on top of a hill near Charlottesville,
Virginia. An image of Jefferson's Monticello is embossed on
the back of the nickel, with Jefferson himself on the front.
Whether the street's name refers to the protection levee or
to Thomas Jefferson's home or both, it is a good choice of
name for the first street inside Jefferson Parish.

A word about the "little mountain," the protection
levee separating Jefferson Parish from Orleans Parish,
is appropriate at this point. Before the huge levees along
the Mississippi River were constructed by the federal
government following the disaster of the great flood of
1927, levees were built locally and by private landowners.
Landowners did not want to sacrifice a lot of fertile, high
land along the river to build levees, and the cost of building
a levee increased with its size. As a result, the levees were
low and relatively small, often shoddy and weak, and
constructed without modern civil-engineering techniques,
which meant they broke with a degree of regularity.

The levee breaks were and still are called by the French

term "crevasse," which means "crack" or "break." When the levee gives way and the river water rushes through the crevasse, much havoc and destruction are wrought. In August 2005, south Louisianians experienced the effects of levee ruptures when hurricane-protection levees failed following Hurricane Katrina. The Mississippi River levee breaks prior to 1927 were similar in the swath of destruction, although the affected population was much smaller. The Sauvé Crevasse was particularly devastating.

On May 3, 1849, the Mississippi River levee gave way on the east bank of Jefferson Parish at the plantation owned by Pierre Sauvé. This crevasse was in the vicinity of what is now **Sauve Road** in River Ridge. The flood waters spread out through the swamps and plantations of east Jefferson and were channeled by the higher land on the Metairie ridge into the city of New Orleans. The flood was the greatest to cover the city until the levee failures following Hurricane Katrina. That flood of 1849 and the fear of future floods from crevasses spurred the construction of protection levees at the parish line. **Monticello Avenue,** therefore, memorializes not only Thomas Jefferson's magnificent home, but also the "little mountain" of the levee that protects New Orleans from crevasse floods.

Before the **Lake Pontchartrain Causeway** was built in the 1950s, the section of what is now **Causeway Boulevard** from the **River Road** north was named **Harlem Avenue.** The name is Dutch, and it comes from the section of New York City that became the home to a large population of African-Americans after the Civil War. The name "Harlem" is from the Dutch word *Haarlem,* an old medieval city in the Netherlands.

Near the **River Road** end of **Causeway Boulevard** is a fortified building that dates from the Civil War. The round-roof structure was a powder magazine supporting the Confederate defensive line called Camp Parapet. The Confederate defenders of New Orleans erected their defenses based on an expected federal assault on the city by

land from upriver. They did not expect federal naval forces
to try to pass heavily fortified and armed Forts St. Philip
and Jackson in Plaquemines Parish on the Mississippi River
below the city. Camp Parapet extended from the Mississippi
River to the point where **Veterans Memorial Boulevard**
now crosses **Causeway Boulevard.** The northerners did
not attack Camp Parapet; they didn't have to. The Union
navy under the command of Commodore David G. Farragut
managed to get past the defenses of Forts St. Philip and
Jackson. When the federal fleet reached New Orleans, there
were no defenders to overcome, and the city surrendered
to the Union. The U.S. Army took over Camp Parapet, and
it became a training center for African-American soldiers
joining the Union army.

After the war, the area around the fort was settled
by freemen, African-American civilians who became a
majority of the population of that part of Jefferson Parish.
There was a degree of local government, with an African-
American justice of the peace and other officials. Inspired
by the bustling African-American community of Harlem in
New York City, the residents of former Camp Parapet called
their main street **Harlem Avenue,** a name that remained
until it was changed to **Causeway Boulevard,** a bland,
generic name without a colorful history, identifying only
with the no-name bridge at the northern end of the street.
With a little knowledge of history and a sense of creativity,
the street namers could have called the wide street Camp
Parapet Boulevard if they didn't like the racial implications
of continuing the name of **Harlem Avenue.** From Dutch
Haarlem to New York's Harlem district to **Harlem Avenue** to
Causeway Boulevard, the neighborhood around the stretch
of **Causeway Boulevard** from Jefferson Highway north to
the railroad tracks remains an African-American enclave of
the parish.

Julius Caesar and other noble Romans of antiquity would
be pleased that there are streets in Jefferson Parish with
names in the Latin language. On the U.S. Coast Guard

station on Grand Isle are **Semper Street and Paratus Place.** The names are taken from the Coast Guard's motto, *Semper Paratus,* meaning "Always Ready." Anyone who studied high school Latin learned that *nova* is the feminine form of the word for "new." Nova is not just a series on public television or a small automobile once made by Chevrolet. **Nova Street** in Terrytown could be named for any or all those meanings; it is part of a cluster of streets whose names begin with *N*.

Intersecting **Metairie Road** in Old Metairie is a street with an interesting name, **Tokalon Place.** The name is from classical Greek, and it means "the beautiful" in the philosophical sense. It could have been written in English as "To Kalon" because το καλον, like English, consists of the word for "beautiful" with the article for "the" preceding it. "Kalon" shows up elsewhere in English in the word "calligraphy," meaning "beautiful writing," and "calliope," "beautiful voice." New Orleans-area residents are familiar with the calliope, a steam-driven musical instrument aboard the SS *Natchez,* the excursion boat on the Mississippi River, blasting out music from the top deck for the amusement of tourists and the annoyance of residents.

There is a series of east-west streets in Metairie that are arranged alphabetically from north to south—sort of. **Fairfield Street** is the first one south of and parallel to **Veterans Memorial Boulevard,** followed by **Garfield, Hastings, Ithaca,** and **Jasper streets.** The *K* street in the series is **Kawanee Avenue.** The name is unusual because it is a word in Malay, a language of Southeast Asia. The meaning of *Kawanee* fits well with the idea of a pleasant residential neighborhood: "friendship." The street's name Kawanee is close to Kewanee in both spelling and pronunciation, but they should not be confused. Kewanee is a town in Illinois whose name comes from a word in the Winnebago Indian language meaning "prairie chicken."

There are other non-English names in the series, including **Ithaca Street,** Greek, named for the mythical island home of Homer's Odysseus; **Utica Street,** from an ancient Phoenician city on the island of Sicily; and **Wabash Street,** an American Indian name of a river and a city in Indiana that means "pure white." Both Ithaca and Utica are also the names of cities in New York. There is also a **Wabash Drive** in Marrero.

There are streets in Jefferson Parish that are named for American Indian tribes. In the Bucktown section of Metairie are **Chickasaw, Cherokee, Huron, Choctaw, Aztec, and Seminole avenues,** as well as **Mayan Lane,** all tribes and languages of North America, if not of Louisiana. Also in Bucktown is **Plaquemine Avenue.** Upriver from Jefferson Parish is the town of Plaquemine and Bayou Plaquemine. Downriver is Plaquemines Parish, usually spoken with a silent *s* consistent with French pronunciation. The name is a French spelling of the word for "persimmon" in the language of the Illinois Indians, a word that found its way down the Mississippi River.

In Old Metairie **Colapissa Street** is located at or near the site of a village of an Indian group by that name. Other Indian tribes and languages are honored in Harvey with **Apache Drive, Inca Drive, Inca Court, Tensas Drive,** and **Ute Drive.**

In River Ridge a driver can turn off **Jefferson Highway** onto **Tullulah Avenue.** The name is best known from actress Tallulah Bankhead, a mid-twentieth-century celebrity who was famous for her throaty drawl and for saying, "Hello, dahling." The spelling of the street's name as "Tullulah" is one vowel off from how Miss Bankhead spelled her name. There is also a town called Tallulah in northeast Louisiana. The origin of "Tallulah" is Choctaw, from a waterfall by that name in Georgia, where Miss Bankhead grew up. It means "leaping waters," thus a waterfall. Whether the name for the street in River Ridge was chosen for the town, the actress, or its Choctaw meaning is unknown. However, it is ominous that a street whose name means "leaping waters" is located not far from the site of the Sauvé Crevasse of 1849. Jefferson Parish doesn't need any more waters leaping through it.

The United Houma Nation of Louisiana, with headquarters in Golden Meadow on Bayou Lafourche, is
honored in the name of **Houma Boulevard** in Metairie. The
word "Houma" is actually only part of the original name
of the tribe, who spoke a Muskogean dialect very close
to Choctaw. The Houma people identified themselves in
a totemic relationship with the red crawfish, *sakti-homa*
in their language. They were the "Red Crawfish" people;
homa, homma, or *houma* means simply "red." There are
many people today in Jefferson, Lafourche, and Terrebonne
parishes who identify themselves as members of the United
Houma Nation. The parish seat of Terrebonne Parish is
the city of Houma. Considering the popularity of eating
crawfish in Louisiana and beyond, there are many people
who are not Houmas who would readily identify themselves
as "red crawfish people."

Choosing a name for anything in a foreign language
can be a tricky, even embarrassing, business. Automobile
manufacturers go to great lengths to choose the name
for a new model, making sure that "Camry" or "Camaro"
does not have any insulting or derogatory connotation or a
double meaning suggesting body parts, physical functions,
or sexual activity in any language where the vehicles might
be sold. The Jefferson Parish Council, the councils of each
incorporated city, and the Louisiana legislature have the
final word on approval of street names, and they usually
keep it clean, although names have slipped through that
have inappropriate meanings in another language. On
Grand Isle is a short street all streets on Grand Isle are
short except **Louisiana Highway 1** with the tongue-in-
cheek name of **Chi Chi Lane**. The term "chichi" is French,
probably originating in the French word "chic," meaning
"stylish" and "elegant." Pronounced *SHEE-SHEE,* the word
means extravagantly stylish, almost gaudy. The houses and
camps on **Chi Chi Lane** are, to say the least, not chichi
at all. In fact, one of the camps has a sign identifying it as
"Fort Apache," not exactly a place where one might see

runway models and jewelry manufacturers. **Chi Chi Lane** leads to a dock where a motorist can buy fresh shrimp right off the boat. No fine clothes or jewels are in sight. There are other meanings to chichi, however.

In September 1944, a young American naval aviator was shot down over the Pacific Ocean, parachuted to the sea, and was rescued by a U.S. Navy submarine. He was Ensign George H. W. Bush, later the president of the United States. The location of this dramatic event was in the Bonin Islands chain, and the nearest island was Chi Chi Jima, north of better-known Iwo Jima. In Japanese, Chi Chi Jima means "Father Island." It is quite improbable that those who named Grand Isle's **Chi Chi Lane** were thinking in Japanese.

If, however, the name "chichi" is considered by someone thinking and speaking in Spanish, the pronunciation and the meaning are different. In Spanish, the word is pronounced *CHEE-CHEE,* and one might think of the famous, flamboyant professional golfer from Puerto Rico, Chi-Chi Rodríguez. In Caribbean Spanish usage, "Chi-Chi" is a nickname, a diminutive term of endearment. Go west of the Caribbean into Mexico and "chichi," still pronounced *CHEE-CHEE,* is a slang term for a woman's breasts.

Driving from **Chi Chi Lane** at the southern end of Jefferson Parish to the northwest corner of the parish next to Lake Pontchartrain in Kenner, you can turn onto **Teton Street.** Its location in a subdivision of streets named for national parks shows that the street was named for the Grand Teton National Park in Wyoming. There is another **Teton Street** in the Estelle community; it, too, is clustered with streets named for western national parks. The French explorers who named the beautiful mountains must have thought they looked like a woman's breasts. *Grand Teton* is the French equivalent of the Mexican *chichi,* with the "grand" emphasizing size. Size mattered to the Frenchmen who gave the beautiful mountains their name.

It is fun to imagine the Jefferson Parish Council in a

humorous, frisky mood when they approved the name of yet another street calling attention to women's chests. In the Nine Mile Point community between Westwego and Bridge City, there is a street named **Hooter Road.** Maybe the council and the developer had shared burgers and a few beers at one of the Hooters restaurants and enjoyed watching the servers in their tight T-shirts? A more likely explanation is that the street is named for someone named Hooter. There was an O. J. Hooter's Furniture store in the Irish Channel of New Orleans, for example, with no connection to the restaurant chain. One wonders if any women living on **Hooter Road** are self-conscious.

In fact, Nine Mile Point, a rather small community, must have been developed by someone with a sense of humor. In addition to **Hooter Road,** there are **Bolo Court, Mono Court,** and **Pato Street.** "Bolo" has many meanings. In police jargon, it is an acronym for "be on the lookout." In the Filipino language Tagalog, it is a large knife or machete. It can also mean a bowling pin or one of those skinny ties made of leather and worn with western wear and square-dance attire. In military slang, a "bolo" is the equivalent of a "bozo," a soldier who doesn't fit into military life. Residents of **Bolo Court**—it is a very short street so there aren't many—have to choose which meaning they will use to explain where they live.

"Mono" comes from the Greek word for "one" or "alone" and shows up in English words such as "monopoly." It is also a short form of the disease mononucleosis, a rather unpleasant name for a residential street. One looks in vain, fortunately, for a Flu Street in Jefferson Parish, the short version of the Italian word "influenza." *Mono* has several meanings in Spanish slang. It can mean a monkey or an addiction or obsession. In Chile, a *mono* is a snowman, and in Mexico it is a leotard. In Spain a *mono* is the coveralls worn by working men.

Those who live on **Pato Street** should know that the name means "duck" in Spanish. But it is also a derogatory term in Spanish slang, meaning a boring, dull person, as well as other unpleasant meanings. A comparison in American English slang is "turkey," translated literally as *pavo* in Spanish. Older maps indicate that there once was a Pavo Street in Nine Mile Point, but no more. Who wants to live on a street named for a turkey? There is no Duck Street in Jefferson Parish, but there is a **Duckhorn Drive** in Marrero (Since when do ducks have horns?) and a **Drake Avenue** just west of Westwego. Quack.

Chapter 6
Old Jefferson

Jefferson Highway begins at the protection levee at the Orleans Parish line and the intersection with **Monticello Avenue.** The highway did not always have that point of origin, that location was not always Orleans Parish, and **Monticello Avenue** did not always have that name. The Town of Carrollton, named for General William Carroll, a hero of the Battle of New Orleans in 1814-1815, was until 1874 part of Jefferson Parish. The Town of Carrollton originally extended upriver to **Labarre Road,** but when it was annexed by the city of New Orleans, the parish line was established at **Monticello Avenue.**

Old maps show that **Monticello Avenue** was named **Upperline Street,** to mark the upriver city limit of the Town of Carrollton. **Lowerline Street,** which still exists in the Carrollton neighborhood of Orleans Parish, was the downriver limit of the town. The name of the street was changed to **Monticello Avenue** in 1924, after the protection levee had been built and after **Jefferson Highway** was opened.

As early as 1871, long before automobiles appeared on the streets of Jefferson Parish, the parish police jury resolved to create a road from **Claiborne Avenue** to **Williams Street** in Kenner. By the second decade of the twentieth century, Kenner was continuing to grow and was a source of farm produce and dairy products for the New Orleans region. To improve the transportation opportunities for residents of the east bank, the Orleans-Kenner Electric Railway Company was created to connect both cities. In 1915 a railway was completed with one terminal at **Canal** and **Rampart streets** in New Orleans and the other sixteen miles upriver in Kenner at the St. Charles-Jefferson parish line. The railroad was called the "O-K Line." Although the railway cars looked very much like the streetcars that still operate on **St. Charles Avenue** in New Orleans, the O-K cars had room for farmers to bring boxes of produce and other products on board to transport to the neighborhood markets in New Orleans.

An act of great foresight by the O-K Line owners led to the creation of **Jefferson Highway** as it is today. When the railway company acquired the land to lay tracks and build stations, it bought a corridor one hundred feet wide, thirty feet for the tracks and thirty-five feet on either side for further use and development. Those buffer and expansion strips would later carry motorized vehicles alongside the railway cars. The O-K Line continued until 1930, when buses replaced them on what had become **Jefferson Highway.**

As motor cars increased in number in the early twentieth century, an association of local developers and boosters was formed to publicize a series of roads that would connect New Orleans and Winnipeg, Canada, more than fifteen hundred miles to the north. In November 1915, the association was formed as the Jefferson Highway Association. The Jefferson Highway Association publicized its connection of roads as the "Pine to Palm" highway.

The highway of 1915 had no resemblance to today's **Jefferson Highway,** except that some of the roads along its route are still in the same location. The original **Jefferson Highway** was a loose connection of local roads, none of them paved, not all of them connected into a unit. The federal highway system did not come into existence until the mid-1920s, so there was no single governmental bureau to plan and maintain the roads. A trip by car from New Orleans to Winnipeg or vice versa took many weeks, with many breakdowns, many mud holes, lots of wrong turns and detours, and speeds seldom exceeding fifteen miles per hour.

In New Orleans the terminus of **Jefferson Highway** was at the intersection of **Common Street** and **St. Charles Avenue**. A plaque marking the highway is still in place at that intersection. The route went out **Common Street** to **Tulane Avenue**, west to **South Carrollton Avenue**, and then turned left. A left turn was necessary because **Jefferson Highway** could not go straight at that point, the future route of **Airline Highway**. In 1915, **Airline Highway** was still twenty years in the future. From its **Carrollton Avenue** leg, **Jefferson Highway** turned right onto **South Claiborne Avenue** and then out to the parish line to where what is known today as **Jefferson Highway** begins. The highway paralleled the O-K Line railway tracks out to Kenner and merged there into **Third Street**, continuing upriver to the St. Charles Parish line, where its route was the same as today's **River Road**. Beyond lay Baton Rouge, where a remnant of **Jefferson Highway** still exists, then the heartland of America and on to Canada.

Old Jefferson today consists of the unincorporated area of east Jefferson bounded by the Orleans Parish line, the Mississippi River, the railroad tracks to the north, and the city of Harahan to the west. Its identity has confused many and apparently continues to do so. For many years it was designated by the United States Postal Service as "New Orleans 21, La." before ZIP codes came into use. Many New Orleanians, with the cheerful parochialism that is part of the city's charm, referred to Old Jefferson as "Metairie" in the belief that *all* of east Jefferson was Metairie. (They didn't even think about Harahan and Kenner.) Eventually "New Orleans 21" became "Jefferson 70121," but by then Ochsner Foundation Hospital and Clinic on **Jefferson Highway** in Old Jefferson had established itself as an internationally recognized medical center in "New Orleans." The institution has never used a "Jefferson" mailing address, and the postal service treats 70121 as New Orleans or Jefferson regardless of the written designation. But it's not Metairie.

A series of streets perpendicular to and ending at

Monticello Avenue show that the people who named them were educated and erudite. The names of the streets are literary figures of long ago, some obscure and forgotten to modern readers of English and American literature. Near the end of **Monticello Avenue** where it terminates at the **River Road** is Pope Street. At first glance, you might think that the street got its name from *the* pope, the man in the Vatican. But when **Pope Street** is considered with its nearby and parallel streets, it is apparent that the Pope of **Pope Street** is the prolific man of letters of the late seventeenth and early eighteenth centuries, Alexander Pope. An Englishman and scholar, Alexander Pope translated Homer's *Iliad* and *Odyssey* into English. He also wrote essays and poems, some of them very long. Many people use the aphorism, "A little knowledge is a dangerous thing," without knowing that it was first written by Alexander Pope.

Addison Street honors and remembers Joseph Addison, an English essayist and dramatist of the seventeenth and eighteenth centuries. Irish writer Oliver Goldsmith was well-known in eighteenth-century England and Ireland for his novel *The Vicar of Wakefield,* still studied today by some English majors if not by members of the Book-of-the-Month Club and neighborhood book groups. He gets a street named after him, too, **Goldsmith Street.**

Back in the days before cigarettes were made with filters, there was a popular brand called Chesterfield. There was also a heavy overcoat with a velvet collar called a Chesterfield, as well as a style of overstuffed sofa with heavy padded arms by that name. But **Chesterfield Street** in Old Jefferson is named for a literary figure from eighteenth-century England, Philip Dormer Stanhope, Fourth Earl of Chesterfield. He was the quintessential English gentleman, for whom good manners were the essence of civilized living. Among his notable writings is a series of letters to his son on the art of becoming a man of the world and a gentleman. Later gentlemen descendents with the same title would popularize the stylish overcoat and the heavy sofa.

Sir Walter Scott, a Scotsman as his name suggests, lived and wrote in the late eighteenth and early nineteenth centuries. He gets an Old Jefferson street dedicated to him, too, and with his first name as well. **Walter Scott Street** shows that the educated street namer was familiar with the author of *Ivanhoe* and a lot of his rhythmic poetry.

A flamboyant and hard-living figure of early eighteenth century England, George Gordon, Lord Byron, wrote poetry that challenged the social standards of the day. In addition to having **Byron Street** named after him, there is a connection, attenuated to be sure, unknown to Byron and most likely to the person who named the street, to Jefferson Parish. In 1814, Byron published a rollicking poem about a pirate called *The Corsair*. Byron had most likely never heard of Jean Lafitte, and it would be almost a year before the privateer, pirate, and organized-crime boss would become a national hero at the Battle of New Orleans. Nevertheless, American readers associated the romantic figure of *The Corsair* with their favorite criminal-hero. It was part of the myth of Jean Lafitte that continues to this day. Lafitte and his henchmen were the rulers of Grand Isle, Grande Terre, and the bayou-laced Barataria region, today all part of Jefferson Parish. Of course, Jefferson Parish did not come into existence until 1825, and by that time Jean Lafitte had disappeared to Galveston, Mexico, and into the mists of myth. Turning from **Monticello Avenue** onto **Byron Street,** a driver might smile and think of *The Corsair* and the colorful buccaneer who left his mark on Jefferson Parish and all of southeastern Louisiana.

The street namers did not skip over the American writers. **Irving Street,** connected to **Monticello Avenue,** honors Washington Irving, one of the greatest American writers of the first part of the nineteenth century. Virtually every American has heard of "Rip Van Winkle" and "The Legend of Sleepy Hollow." Irving also wrote stories under the pseudonym Diedrich Knickerbocker, a name taken from the term for the Dutch settlers of New York and their descendants. The term "knickerbocker" went on to mean a pair of men's trousers that bloused at the knee, ladies' undergarments, and the name of a New York City professional basketball team. There is also an **Irving Street** in the Bissonet Plaza neighborhood of Metairie.

These streets named for literary figures were created in the nineteenth century. On an old map from that period and in real-estate property descriptions, **Gaulding Street,** which is in the nest of streets named for men of letters, is shown to have been originally **Paulding Street.** Why the name was changed to **Gaulding** is not clear. James Kirke Paulding was a collaborator with Washington Irving, for whom nearby **Irving Street** is named, in an early published work of Irving's called *Salmagundi.* It was a collection of essays. The name "Gaulding" however, does not have a similar literary pedigree. Although it is undoubtedly a proper name, a family name, when spelled with a lower-case *g*, "gaulding" means a "rash in the crotch and the inner thighs." Why would anyone name a street after a rash? It sounds gross. The word is best treated as a proper name and written with an upper-case *G*.

Elsewhere in east Jefferson, **Mark Twain Drive** in River Ridge pays homage to a man some call the greatest American writer. Any Americans who have not heard of *Adventures of Huckleberry Finn* and *The Adventures of Tom Sawyer* should leave the country at once after first surrendering their high-school diplomas. These novels are the essence of great American writing. Most readers know that Mark Twain was the pen name of Samuel Langhorne Clemens, but where did Clemens get the name "Mark Twain" and what does it mean?

Henry David Thoreau, nineteenth-century proponent of transcendentalism and author of *Walden*, was the hallowed guru of the hippies of the 1960s and 1970s. But whoever named **Thoreau Street** and its companion, **Walden Drive,** both in River Ridge, could not have been a hippie. The streets were named long before hippies appeared on the scene of American popular culture. The desire to honor Thoreau was most likely due to admiration for his writing and his philosophy. Besides, hippies had other things on their minds than developing a subdivision in River Ridge.

In Terrytown a cluster of streets all begin with the letter *E*. Among them is **Emerson Street,** remembering the famous American philosopher and writer Ralph Waldo Emerson, a leader in the nineteenth-century intellectual movement called transcendentalism.

Most Louisianians have heard of—but probably not read—the long poem *Evangeline,* the sad story of the Acadians being driven from Canada to Louisiana and the separation of the lovers Evangeline and Gabriel. The author of that romantic poetry was Henry Wadsworth Longfellow, who is also known for his rhythmic poem about the Indians of the Great Lakes, *The Song of Hiawatha.* This American poet has a street named for him in the Bissonet Plaza neighborhood, **Longfellow Street.** There is an **Evangeline Street** in Metairie, too.

Nathaniel Hawthorne is another great American writer from the nineteenth century, author of *The Scarlet Letter* and *The House of the Seven Gables.* There is a **Hawthorne Street** on the Westbank near the Timberlane Country Club and a **Hawthorne Avenue** in River Ridge.

Most high-school English teachers introduce their pupils to the writing of Edgar Allan Poe by assigning a reading of the spooky poem, "The Raven." Poe was a prolific writer and poet of the nineteenth century, the master of the short story. His "The Pit and the Pendulum" and "The Fall of the House of Usher," classic horror stories, are still well known and studied today. He died in Baltimore, Maryland, where the home team of the National Football League, the Ravens, took the name of his famous poem. He is not ignored in Jefferson Parish; there is a **Poe Street** in Westwego. No ravens are in residence there, however.

Whoever named a series of streets in the Estelle section of the Westbank had an admiration for some of the great

French men of letters. There are **Hugo Drive, Flaubert Drive, Pascal Drive,** and **Baudelaire Drive.** The first street pays homage to Victor Hugo, best known for *The Hunchback of Notre-Dame* and *Les Misérables.* Gustave Flaubert wrote novels in the nineteenth century and is best known for his then-shocking story of a very selfish woman, *Madame Bovary.* Blaise Pascal was not just a superb writer of the seventeenth century and author of the *Pensées;* he was also a mathematician, philosopher, and mystic. By his own description, Charles Baudelaire's poetry and other writings were raunchy and decadent. His novel, *Les Fleurs du Mal (The Flowers of Evil)* landed him and his publisher in jail for obscenity. Nevertheless, he was a talented writer, but his debauchery shortened his life. Nearby is **Rue Voltaire,** honoring the free-thinking writer of the eighteenth century by calling the street a "rue," which should not be confused with a "roux." Voltaire was the pen name of François-Marie Arouet, whose writings attacked tyranny and repression and contributed an intellectual underpinning to the subsequent French revolution.

Labarre Road begins—or ends—at the Mississippi River in Old Jefferson and goes north to where it is abruptly stopped by railroad tracks. At one time **Labarre Road** crossed the tracks, but that grade crossing was eliminated when **Causeway Boulevard** replaced **Harlem Avenue** and included an overpass above the railroad tracks. North of the tracks **Labarre Road** resumes on the Metairie side. **Labarre Road** crosses **Airline Drive,** then proceeds a few blocks north to its end/beginning at **Metairie Road.** It is one of the oldest streets in east Jefferson and is named for a prominent Jefferson Parish family. New Orleans historian William D. Reeves has written a book about the interesting family and their multigenerational influence on the development of Jefferson Parish: *De La Barre, Life of a French Creole Family in Louisiana.* The de la Barre Family lived in an elegant mansion that is now home to the Magnolia School at the corner of the **River Road** and **Central Avenue.**

Shrewsbury Road, like Labarre Road, begins or ends at the River Road, crosses Jefferson Highway, and stops at the tracks. It, too, once crossed the tracks, but the crossing was eliminated with the construction of the Causeway Boulevard overpass. On the Metairie side of the tracks, Shrewsbury Road ends/begins at the intersection of Airline Drive, Severn Avenue, and Metairie Road. Before Jefferson Highway, Airline Drive, and Severn Avenue were built, Shrewsbury Road was the connection between the River Road and the end of Metairie Road. With Labarre Road, these streets were the only transportation grid in east Jefferson other than trains and boats.

Shrewsbury Road is named for Christian Hardgrave, an Englishman with the title Lord Shrewsbury, a city in England. Lord Shrewsbury was hardly a stuffed-shirt English nobleman. He was something of an adventurer and gadabout. The noble lord was a colleague of William Butler Kenner, a brother of Minor Kenner, the man who established the town of Kennerville that later became the city of Kenner. William B. Kenner was a land speculator who owned the land that he named Shrewsbury to honor his friend. Lord Shrewsbury accompanied Kenner on journeys and adventures. The lord was a man of many manifestations. He has been described as a gambler, a Presbyterian minister, and a hard-drinking lover of whiskey. He was also an impromptu and unconventional educator because, even though it was nominally illegal to do so, he tutored slaves to give them basic literacy.

Lord Shrewsbury's rakish reputation went well with the establishments at his namesake road's intersection with Jefferson Highway in the mid-twentieth century. On one corner was a gas station that provided, like most places in Jefferson in the late 1940s, a one-arm-bandit slot machine. There was a mule farm on another corner, a large operation with a great odor that spread a full block west to Arnoult Road and back toward the River Road. The farm supplied the garbage wagons and Mardi Gras floats in New Orleans with their motive power. There was a greasy-spoon-style restaurant on a third corner, and on the fourth corner was the notorious Crossroads Bar. That establishment had two floors, but only the first floor was a bar. The second floor was a bordello and sporting house.

As sordid as this may seem today, in those times the Crossroads Bar was virtually next door to St. Agnes Church and School. During recess the wimpled nuns and the schoolchildren could have had a good view of the ladies of the evening as they came and went in broad daylight. The structure that housed the church and school until the early 1950s was in keeping with the atmosphere of the rest of the neighborhood. In the building where uniformed children knelt to pray at Mass there had once been gambling tables and nightly entertainment. The gas station, the Crossroads Bar, the mule farm, and the greasy-spoon restaurant are long gone. Another restaurant with digestible food is on that corner. The building that once housed booze and commercial sex has become a dry cleaners. St. Agnes Parish built a new church and school in the 1950s and tore down the old gambling hall. East Jefferson was cleaning up its act. Lord Shrewsbury would probably be disappointed.

Upriver a few blocks from **Shrewsbury Road** was once a horse-racing track. Two brothers, Julius and Morris Hyman, bought up the abandoned race course and laid out a subdivision based on the oval shape of the original track. They at first wanted to celebrate their accomplishment by naming the development Hyman Park, but they decided instead to honor the parish's namesake by calling it Jefferson Park. The main street through the old race track was named **Jefferson Park Avenue**, but they called the outer street on one side of the oval **Hyman Drive**, the other side **Julius Avenue**, and the cross street through the center of the former track **Morris Place**, just so residents wouldn't forget who turned the track into a tract. ("And they're off. . . .")

Across **Jefferson Highway** from **Hyman Drive** is a dead-end street called **Lions Street.** Once upon a time there was a building at the corner of the highway and the street that was the home of the Jefferson Lions Club. Obviously the street behind the club either was not constructed or was not named until the Lions occupied the odd building that was once on that corner. It was odd because its former occupant was a frog farm and cannery. Many years ago frog's legs were a delicacy on restaurant menus and even in home kitchens, but popular tastes are fickle, and the demand for frog's legs declined. The frog farm closed, the Lions replaced the frogs, and the street was named for the Lions. Many years later, the Lions left for a new home on **Causeway Boulevard** that had no history of frogs. The Rio Vista Baptist Church bought the property, tore down the old frog-farm building, and built a new church. A frog-farm barn is not exactly a building that would inspire the faithful to prayer and worship. Besides, the Bible tells a scary story about a plague of frogs in ancient Egypt.

The street is still named for the departed Lions. **Lions Street** makes you think of other streets named for institutions that are no longer around, a Jefferson Parish version of New Orleans's nostalgic lamentation, "Ain't dere no more." In the cluster of streets connected to **Monticello Avenue** and named for literary figures is one named for a definitely nonliterary person, **O'Dwyer Place.** The name of the street comes from a gambling hall, O'Dwyer's Club, that was once at the intersection of **Jefferson Highway** and **Monticello Avenue,** just inside the parish so that New Orleans gamblers did not have to journey far out of their city where the gambling laws were enforced. **O'Dwyer Place** is just behind the Salvation Army Family Store, which now occupies the site of the gamblers' den, an ironic piece of history to be sure.

One block off the **River Road** and crossing **Shrewsbury Road** is a street with the odd name of **Mole Cottage Street.** Most adults can remember reading or hearing the children's classic story of the animals who were good friends and, oh, so British, *The Wind in the Willows* by Kenneth Grahame.

Rat, Badger, and Mole were always, it seems, having tea, with toasts points and honey, and Toad was always causing a commotion with his bad driving. The home of Mole was Mole Cottage, and Grahame's description makes it one of the coziest places ever. Walt Disney adapted *The Wind in the Willows* and made it into an animated film called *The Adventures of Ichabod and Mr. Toad.* In Britain today there are bed-and-breakfast places with the name Mole Cottage. Old Jefferson's **Mole Cottage Street** has no bed-and-breakfast and would not be described as cozy, but the name brings up pleasant childhood memories.

In a remote edge of Old Jefferson, just west of **Central Avenue** and hard against the embankment supporting the railroad approach to the **Huey P. Long Bridge,** is a street named for a conservative Republican U. S. senator from New Hampshire, **Senator Tobey Street.** The connection between Senator Charles Tobey and Jefferson Parish is illegal gambling. Gambling halls and slot machines were open and notorious in Jefferson Parish in the postwar 1940s. The best known was the elegant Beverly Country Club at the corner of **Labarre Road** and **Jefferson Highway.** There were others along **Monticello Avenue;** barrooms and gas stations had slot machines, too. Gambling was, of course, officially illegal, but the laws were not enforced. U. S. Senator Estes Kefauver of Tennessee helped put an end to all of that with the hearings and evidence before the Special Committee to Investigate Organized Crime in Interstate Commerce, of which he was chairman. During the hearings in Washington, D.C., one of the first such hearings on live television, testimony revealed that New York gangster Frank Costello had business connections with a Jefferson Parish resident, Carlos Marcello, reputed to be the mafia boss of Louisiana. Marcello and Costello owned one or more of the gambling halls in Jefferson Parish, according to evidence presented to the committee. This hearing was reality television before the concept was invented, and Americans watched in great numbers.

Senator Tobey was a vocal member of the Kefauver committee. He had been in the senate for many years, and he was a crusty, plain-spoken Yankee. Although he had enjoyed cordial friendship with Democratic President Franklin D. Roosevelt, the New Hampshire Republican was an opponent of Roosevelt's package of government programs known as the New Deal. In fact, in 1940, Senator Tobey declared the New Deal "a disaster." Very much a man of the "old school," Tobey wore a green eyeshade and pressed the witnesses before the committee hard for evidence of organized crime's pervasiveness. Whoever named the modest street in Old Jefferson must have been an admirer. By the time Senator Tobey died in 1953, gambling in Jefferson Parish was being shut down, in large part because of the revelations before the senate committee. The senator left behind several memorable quotations including, "The two great enemies within our ranks, the criminals and the communists, often work hand in hand. Wake up, America!" Those who live on **Senator Tobey Street** have no difficulty waking up; next to their street is the point where the locomotives start climbing up the grade on the approach to the **Huey P. Long Bridge,** with diesels throbbing and cars shifting.

The **Huey P. Long Bridge** has one end in Old Jefferson and the other in appropriately named Bridge City. Louisiana's most famous (some would say infamous, too) governor was assassinated a few months before the bridge that bears his name was opened in 1935. At the base of the vehicular part of the bridge on the east bank is where the defining line of Old Jefferson starts to get fuzzy. **Clearview Parkway**—one of those bland, pleasant-sounding street names with no historical reference that means little—is the wide thoroughfare from the bridge, through Old Jefferson and Metairie, and all the way to Lake Pontchartrain. However, the large commercial and industrial sections of Old Jefferson upriver from **Clearview Parkway** are on the site of the Elmwood Plantation, and the area is usually called "Elmwood" rather than "Old Jefferson." **Elmwood Park Boulevard** is one of the principal streets through the industrial section of Elmwood. The Elmwood Plantation manor house has burned at least twice during its long history, and the last time that happened the house was not rebuilt. **Elmwood Park Boulevard,** thus, is another street honoring a structure that, "Ain't dere no more." Because the Elmwood area is between **Clearview Parkway** and the city of Harahan, many people consider it part of Harahan even though it is outside that city's limits. Fortunately, the post office and private delivery services usually recognize that Elmwood addresses may be written Jefferson, Harahan, or even New Orleans, and the goods get to the right places.

During World War II, the U.S. Army had established at Elmwood a receiving and training facility on the land that would become today's commercial and industrial zone. Spreading over more than four hundred acres, it was called Camp Plauché in honor of Jean Baptiste Plauché, the leader of the New Orleans uniformed militia at the Battle of New Orleans in 1814-15. Major Plauché also served as Louisiana's lieutenant governor from 1850 to 1853. Camp Plauché was decommissioned in 1946, and the barracks and other buildings became postwar housing. Part of the camp was used by Ochsner Foundation Hospital until its permanent facility on Jefferson Highway was built in the 1950s. Plauché and the camp named for him are remembered by the names of **Plauche Street** and **Plauche Court** in the Elmwood Industrial Park, usually written without the French acute accent.

You should not expect a short cut or any other way of saving time on **Time Saver Avenue** in Elmwood. The street is named for a chain of convenience stores, the first such stores in the New Orleans area. The corporate headquarters was the first in that industrial section of Elmwood and had the street named for the company.

Old Jefferson is separated from Metairie mostly by railroad tracks. Alongside those tracks, sometimes over the tracks, is the elevated **Earhart Expressway.** It is an extension of **Earhart Boulevard** in New Orleans, and the expressway begins at the parish line and heads westward to its end at **Dickory Avenue**, across that street from **Mouse Lane.** The **Earhart Expressway** and its origin, **Earhart Boulevard**, are named for a New Orleans politician, Fred A. Earhart. He was a pharmacist and a leader of the Regular Democratic Organization, known in political circles as "The Old Regulars." Earhart served as mayor of New Orleans for one day, July 15, 1936, after Mayor T. Semmes Walmsley resigned and before Mayor Robert Maestri took office. During the Maestri administration, Earhart served as commissioner of public utilities.

Does Jefferson Parish have a center? The parish spreads south from Lake Pontchartrain across the Mississippi River through the Westbank and the watery Barataria region to Grand Isle and the Gulf of Mexico. It is difficult to point to any spot on the map that might be considered a center. Any such difficulty was ignored by those who found centers throughout the parish and named streets accordingly. **Central Avenue** in Old Jefferson is the center, sort of, of that neighborhood, extending from **Airline Drive** south to the **River Road** at the Mississippi River levee. But there is a **Central Avenue** in the town of Jean Lafitte, too, and a **Central Boulevard** in Harvey. Westwego has its own **Central Avenue**, and there is a **Central Drive** in Metairie. Two more streets named **Central Avenue** are in Gretna and the Chênière Caminada community across the bridge from Grand Isle. The latter street is divided by **Louisiana Highway 1** into **East** and **West Central** avenues. On Grand Isle itself, at just about the middle of the island, is a tiny street with the grand name **Central Parkway.** In Waggaman, **Center Street** could be considered, with some leeway, the center of the Kennedy Heights subdivision, but **Center Street** in Metairie does not seem to be the center of anything. Maybe all these streets named "Central" and "Center" are a reflection that many Jeffersonians consider their homes to be the center of the world.

Trivia answer: Clemens worked on a Mississippi River steamboat. To determine whether the water was deep enough for the boat, a deckhand would toss a weighted line over the side. Two fathoms (twelve feet) of water was the safe depth for navigation. When the sounding showed that depth, the sailor would call out to the pilot house, "Mark twain," "twain" being an old word for "two."

Chapter 7
Go, Saints!

S outh Louisiana is full of saints. The Catholic culture and the history of the region are reflected in the many place and street names dedicated to saints of the Catholic Church. Civil parishes took on the names of the geographical Catholic parishes rather than counties, like the other states of the Union. And, of course, there are the region's football heroes, the New Orleans Saints, world champions and winners of Super Bowl XLIV on February 7, 2010. Jefferson Parish has not exempted itself from honoring the holy men and women and has dedicated many streets in their names and honor.

In the northwest section of Kenner, there is a cluster of streets all named for saints. These names were given at the time St. Elizabeth Ann Seton Church and Parish were being established by the Archdiocese of New Orleans in response to the increased Catholic population in rapidly growing north Kenner. The saints' streets surround St. Elizabeth's Church, with one understandably named **St. Elizabeth Drive** and another **Seton Boulevard.** St. Elizabeth was an American who lived in New York in the early part of the nineteenth century. She was a widow; her husband died in Italy where he went because of failing health. She sought a deeper relationship with God and founded an order of nuns, the Daughters of Charity of the United States. St. Elizabeth is much revered by many American Catholics.

St. Paul Drive in Kenner is named for one of the best-known saints, the man most responsible for the spread of Christianity beyond the Jewish world after the death of

Jesus. His influence spread so far, they named the capital city of Minnesota for him. He is also known in River Ridge, especially on **St. Paul Avenue.**

Every February 3, Catholics observe the feast of St. Blaise by getting their throats blessed. The saint is the patron of diseases of the throat. In Kenner the saint's name is spelled with no *i* on **St. Blase Drive,** and the residents of that street can observe the saint's day every day.

The legendary patron saint of travelers has a street in Kenner also, **St. Christopher Drive.** The Church no longer celebrates the feast of St. Christopher. He was officially "de-canonized" by the Vatican purge of inauthentic saints during the 1960s, some of whom had been venerated for centuries. Research disclosed that many saints, including St. Christopher, were a manifestation of old stories and legends that had been passed down over generations with no historical basis in an actual holy person who was once alive. Another patron of travelers, not as well known as St. Christopher and also legendary, is named in **St. Julien Drive.** St. Julian the Hospitaller was a martyr of the early Christian church, but his authenticity is somewhat questionable. No matter. He is honored by the street in Kenner. Or **St. Julien Drive** could be considered to honor St. Julien du Mans, another legendary French saint. He was said to be the first bishop of Le Mans in the third or fourth century.

Kenner remembers St. Ann, the mother of Mary and grandmother of Jesus, in **St. Ann Drive.** She gives her name also to **St. Ann Street** in Marrero. Marrero's Vietnamese community persuaded the Jefferson Parish Council to name the street near their church **St. Le Thi Thanh Street.** St. Agnes Le Thi Thanh was a mother of six children and was martyred in eighteenth-century Vietnam during a horrible persecution that killed thousands of Catholics.

There are lots of saints named John, so residents of Kenner's **St. John Drive** can pick which St. John they wish to remember or honor or whose grace and inspiration they invoke. St. John the Apostle, St. John the Baptist, St. John the Evangelist, St. John of the Cross, St. John Chrysostom, St. John Bosco, St. John Vianney, and many more including St. John the Dwarf are officially canonized saints.

St. James Drive, in the group of streets around St. Elizabeth Ann Seton Church, can also refer to multiple saints. There were two of Jesus' twelve apostles named James, one being called St. James Major, the other St. James the Less.

There was more than one St. Bridget, which gives the residents of **St. Bridget Drive** near St. Elizabeth's Church some flexibility. St. Bridget or Brigid or Bride or Brigit is a legendary patron of Ireland who may have lived in the sixth century as an abbess. Some historians are not sure whether she was an actual person or is more a personification of old tales and legends. There is historical evidence for St. Bridget of Sweden, a holy woman of the fourteenth century.

There are many saints named Thomas: Thomas the Apostle (Doubting Thomas); Thomas à Kempis, medieval writer of meditations; Thomas Aquinas, one of the most important theologians in Christianity; Thomas Becket, murdered by King Henry II in his cathedral at Canterbury; and several more. Those who live on **St. Thomas Drive** in Kenner can pick and choose which Thomas is theirs.

For which St. Francis was **St. Francis Street** in Metairie named? St. Francis of Assisi is the best-known St. Francis, but there are St. Francis Xavier, St. Francis de Sales, St. Francis Borgia, and others as well.

St. Michael Drive is near the West Jefferson Medical Center in Harvey and is named for the archangel who is the patron saint of soldiers. St. Michael was the leader of the forces of angels who defeated Lucifer and the evil angels, sending them to hell for eternity.

St. Joseph, husband of Mary and patron of Sicily and the St. Joseph's altars, has three streets in Jefferson Parish named in his honor. There are a **St. Joseph Street** and a **St. Joseph Lane** in Harvey, both close to the Harvey Canal. Another **St. Joseph Street** is in the Little Farms neighborhood of River Ridge.

In Westwego there is a street named for an obscure saint who is identified with a cathedral town in the Lorraine valley of France, **St. Die Street.** St. Dié's name was long ago abbreviated from the French St. Dieudonné, which is translated from the Latin name St. Deodatus, meaning "given by God." Another obscure French saint's name is given to a street in Terrytown, **Rue St. Honore.** St. Honoré was a legendary bishop of Amiens, France, in the early seventh century. He left his name on a street and neighborhood in Paris, France.

Next to **Rue St. Honore** in Terrytown is a street named for one of the best-known French kings, **Rue St. Louis XIV.** Making King Louis XIV a saint in Terrytown is either a joke or a mistake. *That* King Louis was no saint. He lived lavishly and extravagantly, suppressed the peasants, and kept mistresses, not exemplary behavior that is usually considered to be holy and sacramental. Louis XIV is the king from whom Louisiana gets its name, thanks to René-Robert Cavelier, Sieur de La Salle, who sailed down the Mississippi River in 1682 and made claim to all the land drained by the river in the name of his king. Perhaps the intent was to name the street for another king named Louis, St. Louis, King of France and patron saint of Louisiana and New Orleans, but that king was Louis IX, not Louis XIV. Maybe someone forgot how to count in Roman numerals.

Continuing the theme of French saints in that Terrytown neighborhood, there is the **Avenue Mont Martre,** named for the hill in Paris where the picturesque Basilica of the Sacred Heart *(Sacre Coeur)* is located. The name means the "Mountain of Martyrs," because long ago some Christians, including Saint Denis, were murdered there.

A preceding chapter discussed the Spanish street names in the Rio Vista neighborhood of Old Jefferson. They are saints, too. **San Mateo Avenue** is St. Matthew, a tax collector who became an apostle and gospel writer. **Santa Ana Avenue** is St. Ann, and **San Jose Avenue** is St. Joseph. **San Carlos Avenue** is St. Charles Borromeo, archbishop of

The Vatican didn't canonize King Louis XIV, but Terrytown did.

Milan, for whom neighboring St. Charles Parish is named. St. Rose is the English for **Santa Rosa Avenue,** the holy woman of Lima, Peru. The community of St. Rose, next door to Kenner on the **River Road,** is named for her.

Drivers on busy **Causeway Boulevard** in Metairie may notice a sign marking **St. Rene Street.** It commemorates the Frenchman René Goupil, killed by the Iroquois on September 23, 1642, in what is now upstate New York. He was the first of a group of Jesuit missionaries identified as the North American martyrs. St. René was a Jesuit brother whose mission among the Huron people was caring for the sick and injured. He is the patron saint of anesthetists, most likely because his own death by torture was so gruesome and painful.

Loyola Drive and its east and west branches are the principal streets of the University City neighborhood of Kenner. Although the street was named for Loyola University in New Orleans, the name refers to St. Ignatius of Loyola, a Basque soldier who founded the Society of Jesus, the Jesuits.

The upriver edge of the Jefferson Heights subdivision in Old Jefferson is **St. George Street.** St. George is famous in legend for slaying dragons, and little factual information is known about him other than that he was a martyr in the early Christian church. Somehow over centuries he got to be associated with chivalry and knighthood, and he became and still is the patron saint of England. In Old Jefferson his street is a reminder that the St. George Plantation once was located near where the **Huey P. Long Bridge** now stands.

St. Martin Street, situated in Metairie, and **Rue St. Martin** in Kenner are named for St. Martin of Tours, a Roman soldier who is often pictured in stained-glass windows and other art cutting his cloak in half and offering it to a beggar. One block away from **St. Martin Street** is **St. Mary Street.** There are many saints named Mary, but for most Christians, especially Catholics and Eastern Orthodox, the name Mary means Mary the Virgin, the mother of Jesus. The patron saint of battered women, St. Rita of Cascia, has a street named for her in Marrero, **St. Rita Street.**

In the Estelle neighborhood lies **St. Jude Street.** The choice of this saint for the name of a residential street is disconcerting. On the one hand, there are many people who find great comfort in their devotion to St. Jude, one of the twelve apostles. On the other hand, St. Jude is the patron saint of hopeless cases and impossible results, not exactly the mood that should prevail on a quiet, sedate residential street. Once there was a hospital in Kenner named for St. Jude. How did sick or injured patients feel, already in stress and anxious, when the ambulance pulled into a place dedicated to the patron of hopeless cases? One could feel equally uneasy turning off the **Leo Kerner-Lafitte Parkway** onto **St. Jude Street** to shop for a house. However, there is a connecting street dedicated to one or many of the saints named John, **St. John Drive,** and there is a **St. John Avenue** a little farther north in Marrero.

Farther south in the Barataria community there is **St. Anthony Street**, named for the Catholic church across Bayou Barataria in the town of Jean Lafitte, St. Anthony of Padua.

A small, busy street connects busy **Hickory Avenue** with busier **Jefferson Highway** near Harahan city hall. Named for a Harahan family who owns a truck and auto repair shop and has been active in the business and political life of Harahan, **St. Cyr Street** presents a study in how the name of a legendary holy child can come to have many different meanings to different people through many centuries. The original story is very ancient. A pious Christian widow named Julitta was attempting to escape persecution and fled with her three-year-old son, Cyricus, to Tarsus, the hometown of St. Paul. But she and the boy were caught, tortured, and killed, becoming martyrs. Local Christians saved their relics, and some of these found their way to France. There the story involves the ninth-century Emperor Charlemagne having a dream in which a child appears riding on a wild boar and saves the emperor from death. The dream was interpreted as a vision of St. Cyricus, also known as Quiricus, Cyriacus, and Cyr. The cathedral in the city of Nevers was dedicated to St. Cyr because of the inspiration of the emperor's dream.

As with many European family names, St. Cyr became associated not only with the legendary saint himself but with the town, the region, and the people who lived there. Families named St. Cyr immigrated to North America and spread. Being French and having an elegant, sophisticated cachet when spoken or written, the name was adopted for the stage by a burlesque performer who became famous in the 1940s and 1950s for removing her clothing in public to the beat of a drum, Lili St. Cyr. The real St. Cyr family should take some solace in knowing that Lili was not by birth or marriage one of their own.

Meanwhile, back in France, Napoleon Bonaparte had established a school for training professional military

officers at the town of Saint-Cyr-l'École near the estate
of Versailles. The official name of the school was École
Spéciale Militaire de Saint-Cyr. The shorthand name
became simply "St. Cyr," the French military academy, just
as "West Point" and "Sandhurst" became the short names
of the United States Military Academy and Britain's Royal
Military Academy, respectively. After World War II, St. Cyr
was moved from the town of that name west to Brittany,
but the official name of the school for professional soldiers
continues to be Saint-Cyr.

From a legendary child saint to an emperor's dream to
a military school to a far-flung family to a 1940s stripper
to a little street in Harahan, St. Cyr has come a long way
from the young boy who was murdered by persecutors
in ancient Greece. **St. Cyr Street** is so short and so busy
a driver should not think about any of this history and
legend while guiding a vehicle from **Jefferson Highway** to
Hickory Avenue, especially not any mental images of Lili
St. Cyr removing her garments for the amusement of her
customers.

All the saints, just as on All Saints Day, are remembered
by **Saints Drive** in Metairie, one block off **Airline Drive**
near the Mike Miley Playground. The street was so named
because the New Orleans Saints football team had its
practice facility there before the larger structure was built
on **Airline Drive** near Zephyr Field. All the saints in heaven
and in Jefferson Parish were cheering on February 7, 2010,
when the Saints won the Super Bowl for the first time.
Saints make people believe in miracles.

Chapter 8

Don Quixote on the Bayou

Barataria Boulevard is the longest named street in Jefferson Parish. It begins at the Mississippi River levee in Marrero and proceeds directly south for three miles before turning slightly to the west. This turn is just past **Eighty Arpent Road,** and the turn marks the point at which the street begins to parallel the vestigial remnant of Bayou des Familles. That old bayou was once a part of the Mississippi River, cut off centuries ago and now reduced to little more than a drainage ditch for several miles in Marrero and Estelle. It was called Bayou Barataria and Little Bayou Barataria at times before the name Bayou des Familles took hold.

Barataria Boulevard follows the bayou south of Estelle, through the floodwall of the hurricane-protection levee, and into the Barataria Preserve of the Jean Lafitte National Historical Park and Preserve. After passing through the preserve, **Barataria Boulevard** crosses **Leo Kerner-Lafitte Parkway** into the community of Crown Point. The roadway makes a sharp turn to the south as it approaches Bayou Barataria, which is part of the Gulf Intracoastal Waterway, and parallels that bayou for a few miles until it ends at the small community of Jones Point and the southern end of the Barataria Preserve. It is a road with a lot of history and tales to tell, beginning with its name.

Early French maps of the region show a place identified as the Isle Barataria in the general vicinity of the confluence of what are now called Bayou Barataria and Bayou Villars. The first European landowner and surveyor was Claude-Joseph Villars Dubreuil Sr., who acquired the land in the

1730s or earlier. It was most likely he who gave the name "Barataria" to a plot of land that wasn't really an island, just a higher place in the swamp that could support some grazing cattle. Monsieur Dubreuil read what novels were available in that early period in Louisiana because there was a copy of Miguel de Cervantes's *Don Quixote* in his library. At that time the novel was very popular in France, having been translated into French from the Spanish in 1614. In that story, one of the greatest novels ever written, Sancho Panza, the squire-companion to the mad, would-be knight Don Quixote, is briefly made the governor of a fictional island called Barataria. Governor Panza's fantasy island was not a true island because it was not completely surrounded by water. The name of the island is most likely a pun in the Spanish language of the early seventeenth century. Cervantes was using his novel as a form of satire and social commentary on the attitudes of his time, a contrast of idealism and cynicism. Don Quixote imagined himself to be a noble knight-errant; Sancho Panza imagined himself to be a governor. Cervantes frequently used word play and puns to highlight the parody. "Barataria" is a word in Old Provençal, a language of the Provence region of southern France. It means "fake," "deceptive," or "fraudulent." It was a fitting name for the "island" of Barataria, which was a fake island for Sancho to govern.

It is thus likely that Monsieur Dubreuil observed a plot of land that was part of an old alluvial ridge along what later became known as Bayou Barataria and was more or less surrounded by other small bayous. He thought that this island that wasn't quite an island deserved the name of Sancho Panza's gubernatorial realm. The name became popular, and the bayou acquired the name, too. It had been called the Bayou of the Ouachas, named for an Indian group who had lived in the region but who disappeared shortly after the arrival of Europeans. A European settlement in the vicinity became known as "Barataria," too, then the broad body of water to the south, and eventually the entire region.

There was no **Barataria Boulevard** along the current route of that roadway in the colonial years, but there was a road built at least as early as when Spain owned Louisiana that followed a route along the east side of Bayou des Familles from the point near the Mississippi River where that bayou and Bayou Barataria began as distributary channels. That Barataria Road was called *Chemin de Barataria* in French and *El Camino Real de Barataria* in Spanish. Part of that road has become hiking trails in the Barataria Preserve of the Jean Lafitte National Historical Park.

In 1895, a dirt road was built from what is now Marrero to Bayou Barataria along the west side of Bayou des Familles near the current route of **Barataria Boulevard.** A ferry transported travelers across Bayou Barataria. The road was frequently impassable when rain turned the dirt to mud, and there were no automobiles on the road until 1915. The road was extended five miles south to Lafitte in 1923. It was difficult and treacherous driving to say the least.

There was no place named Marrero in 1895. The unincorporated area was known as Amesville, the name originating in the Ames Plantation that once occupied that expanse of land. **Ames Boulevard,** which stretches from **Fourth Street** south across **Barataria Boulevard** through Estelle, preserves the memory of Amesville and the Ames Plantation. Amesville became Marrero in 1908 and is named for the energetic businessman and politician Louis H. Marrero Sr. Marrero was a Confederate veteran of the Civil War, banker, landowner and developer, police juror, president of the police jury, member of the levee board, and long-serving sheriff of Jefferson Parish. In addition to the community being named for him, Marrero is also memorialized by **Marrero Road,** which is located where his principal land holdings were established between **Ames Boulevard** and **Barataria Boulevard.**

Is there a word to identify the people who live in Marrero? Are they Marreronians or Marreronans or Marrerish? The change from Amesville to Marrero has at least kept them

from being known as the Ameish and being confused with
the Amish people, sometimes called the Pennsylvania
Dutch.

Eighty Arpent Road, which crosses **Barataria Boulevard**
in Marrero, evokes in its name some interesting history of
land measurement. The period when Louisiana was a colony
of France, from 1682, when explorer René-Robert Cavelier,
Sieur de La Salle, claimed the entire Mississippi Valley for
Louis XIV, until 1763, when France gave Louisiana to Spain
in a treaty, was well before the institution of the metric system
in Europe. The English system of land measurement—feet,
inches, and so forth—was not used in French or Spanish
Louisiana. Land along the Mississippi River was surveyed
in long lots, measured parallel to the river and extending
back to the swamp or marsh to a depth of forty or eighty
arpents. The unit of measure was the French arpent, which
is both a square and a linear measurement. A linear arpent
is not quite 193 feet, which means that eighty arpents from
the front of the property along the river extends to a depth
of 15,360 feet, or just short of three miles. **Eighty Arpent
Road** marks that distance.

South of Estelle on **Barataria Boulevard,** just before
the hurricane-protection levee and the entrance to the
Barataria Preserve, is St. Joachim's Catholic Church. Across
the road from the church is a street called **Merlin Lane.** At
first look it seems odd that a street named for the pagan
sorcerer in the legend of King Arthur would be juxtaposed
to a Catholic church. However, **Merlin Lane** is one of three
parallel adjacent streets intersecting **Barataria Boulevard**
that are named for falcons. A merlin is occasionally seen
in coastal Louisiana and feeds on small birds. The other
nearby streets are **Peregrine Lane** and **Kestrel Lane,** two
other species of falcons.

By the 1930s many automobiles and trucks were
reaching the Barataria country all the way to the Lafitte
community at the end of the road. In those days, progress
was identified with building more roads to connect

previously isolated communities that could be reached only by boats. Plans were begun to construct a road from Lafitte through the swamps and marsh to Larose on Bayou Lafourche, the point where that bayou and the Intracoastal Waterway intersect. The road would roughly parallel the relatively new Gulf Intracoastal Waterway and become an engine for economic development. Officials of Jefferson Parish, the state of Louisiana, and the federal government enthusiastically supported the idea of a road connecting Lafitte and Larose.

World War II presented more important challenges than building a road through the Barataria wetlands, but the idea was kept alive. By the 1960s Jefferson Parish and the entire nation were engaged in building roads everywhere. Every family, it seemed, had at least one automobile, and trucks were challenging railroads as the means of getting goods to the marketplace quickly. The Eisenhower Interstate Highway System was laying miles of road through the country on a daily basis. Jefferson Parish was expanding, too. There was no room for development to the north, east, or west because the parish's boundaries were established by Lake Pontchartrain, Orleans Parish, and St. Charles Parish. There were, however, broad open spaces on the Westbank south of the **Westbank Expressway.** There had long been communities at Crown Point, Jones Point, Barataria, and Lafitte, and there was lots of open land, mostly woods and swamp, in between. To open all that Westbank land for development, more roadways were needed in addition to **Barataria Boulevard.**

The enthusiasm for a road connecting **Barataria Boulevard** with the community of Larose grew through the 1960s, and the Westbank continued to expand. After the completion of the **Westbank Expressway**—at least the ground-level roadway—in 1957, another broad throughway, parallel to the river and the expressway but farther south, was in the works. That street would eventually extend from the Orleans Parish line westward to Highway 90 and ran alongside the high-voltage lines on tall towers owned by the Louisiana Power and Light Company. It was called **Lapalco Boulevard,** probably the only street in the parish named with an acronym. That power company is now defunct, which means that the boulevard is among those named for something that "ain't dere no more." The power lines remain, carrying electricity across the Westbank and then over the Mississippi River and along the aptly named **Powerline Drive** in Old Jefferson at the edge of Harahan, then north into Metairie and along **Power Boulevard** to Lake Pontchartrain.

With the completion of **Lapalco Boulevard,** there was more pressure for development south of it and new roads to support the expansion. Yet another trans-Westbank road was in the planning stage, and it was to be a limited-access highway and part of the Interstate system. It was tentatively numbered Interstate 29 and would be known by a real name, the Dixie Freeway. The vision of the road planners was that the Dixie Freeway would begin on its west end at **Interstate 10** in St. Charles Parish west of Kenner. It would sweep south, cross the Mississippi River on a new bridge that would become the **Hale Boggs Memorial Bridge,** and then eastward, crossing **Highway 90,** and proceed through the wetlands to somewhere between Estelle and Crown Point. From there, Interstate 29 would continue eastward into Plaquemines Parish, cross the river to Chalmette in St. Bernard Parish on a new bridge, and connect again with **Interstate 10** in the eastern part of Orleans Parish. The proposal was breathtaking and would mimic the beltways of Interstate highways around other major cities.

By the 1970s, however, environmentalists and preservationists were beginning to question the need for all these roads, whether they were economically justified, and how much damage they would be doing to the wetlands. Preservationists in New Orleans had, through litigation, stopped the construction of proposed Interstate 310, part of which would have been an elevated expressway along the riverfront in the Vieux Carré. The highway mileage allotted to that project was transferred to the Dixie Freeway and designated Interstate 410. Even before construction began, the Dixie Freeway came crashing down, too, when federal highway officials could not justify the cost and environmental damage. Two pieces of it were constructed, however. **Interstate 310** begins at **Interstate 10** just west of Kenner, as originally proposed. It heads south, crosses the Mississippi River on the **Hale Boggs Bridge,** and ends at **Highway 90** in Boutte. Another section from **Interstate 10** in eastern New Orleans proceeds south to **Chef Menteur Highway, Highway 90.**

The long-proposed road from Lafitte to Larose came under the scrutiny of that period. In 1974, the town of Jean Lafitte on the east side of Bayou Barataria was incorporated as the population of that section of the Barataria region increased. There were political fights and litigation over the proposed road, proposed residential development, and the proposed Jean Lafitte National Park. The Clean Water Act was being used successfully to limit development and protect wetlands. The Des Familles Development Corporation's plans for a residential development in an environmentally sensitive area were checked by litigation. But the pressure to build the roadway, which had come to be called the **Lafitte-Larose Highway,** continued until 1977, when the Louisiana State Highway Department withdrew its federal application under the Clean Water Act to build the final phase of the road from Wagner's Ferry Bridge at Bayou Barataria to **Highway 308** on Bayou Lafourche at Larose. That meant that the **Lafitte-Larose Highway** would not even reach Lafitte, let alone Larose. What was left of the highway project was completed in 1977 and crosses Bayou Barataria, the Intracoastal Waterway, in a high-rise bridge and then ends abruptly in a hairpin loop that brings a driver back 180 degrees to **Jean Lafitte Boulevard.** A few miles south is the town of Jean Lafitte and even farther is the unincorporated community of Lafitte. From the top of the bridge a driver can look off into the marsh and envision the road that never was.

At one point in 2002, there was an effort to rename the **Lafitte-Larose Highway** the Des Familles Parkway, but the legislature did not take up the measure. In 2004, the legislature did approve a name change, almost thirty years after the road was built reaching neither Lafitte nor Larose and thus never living up to its name, to the **Leo Kerner-Lafitte Parkway**. Leo Kerner was the first and long-time mayor of the town of Jean Lafitte, a vigorous and vocal proponent for what he thought was good for his constituents. The road still doesn't go to Lafitte or even to the town of Jean Lafitte, but it does parallel and then bisect the Barataria Preserve of the Jean Lafitte National Historical Park and Preserve.

The name of Jean Lafitte is on many streets and places in the Barataria region. In addition to the national park, the community of Lafitte, and the town of Jean Lafitte, the name of the principal roadway, **Louisiana Highway 45,** on the east side of Bayou Barataria is **Jean Lafitte Boulevard.** There are businesses that use the legendary corsair's name, and the road on the west side of Bayou Barataria running through the Barataria community is **Privateer Boulevard.** In the Estelle community there is a residential street connected to **Barataria Boulevard** named **Pirates Alley** in recognition of the criminal activities of Jean Lafitte and his organization, but probably also a copy of **Pirate Alley** alongside St. Louis Cathedral in the Vieux Carré of New Orleans. Among other endeavors besides piracy, Jean Lafitte and his association of smugglers and raiders were privateers, meaning that they had legal authority from a nation-state to, in effect, commit acts of piracy upon the ships of another country with whom the country authorizing the raiding was at war. Lafitte's legal authority was a letter of marque from the short-lived Republic of Cartagena on the Caribbean coast of what would later become the nation of Colombia. Lafitte's henchmen did not always limit their high-seas pillaging to the ships of Spain, against whom Cartagena was rebelling. It was not unusual for the Lafitte organization to capture merchant vessels of opportunity, which was simply piracy. Captured goods were eagerly sought by the well-to-do people of New Orleans and the Mississippi River plantations and towns, the goods were otherwise not available. Like Americans today, they didn't like to pay taxes, and smuggled goods are by definition tax free. Before Jefferson Parish existed and before there were good roads, the bayous and canals of the Barataria region provided many ways to reach customers from Lafitte's headquarters on Grand Isle and Grande Terre.

Jean Lafitte and his people became national heroes because of their assistance to General Andrew Jackson in the Battle of New Orleans. President James Madison issued pardons to them for their contributions, and Jean Lafitte and his band entered into folklore and legend as heroes. The people who live in the town of Jean Lafitte and along **Jean Lafitte Boulevard** have the distinction of living in a town and region named for an organized-crime boss who was a national hero.

Chapter 9
Scaling the Heights

Jefferson Parish is flat. Very, very flat. The land on both sides of the Mississippi River was formed several thousand years ago by silt being deposited into what would be named the Gulf of Mexico. Periodically the meandering river would overflow and spread silt-heavy water beyond its natural banks. As the flowing water decreased in velocity, the suspended sand and soil dropped out. The next flood added more, and the process repeated again and again over hundreds of years. Vegetation sprouted; trees took root. More floods came and continued to raise the level of the land. Along the banks near the actual course of the river, the silt was deposited higher than it was farther away because, as the moving water overflowed the banks, it slowed suddenly and substantially, dropping most of its suspended silt closest to the channel. These natural levees were the highest places in the newly created land, banks which were substantial enough to support large trees.

Every now and then through the centuries, the river's crest would be so high and the flow so great that the natural levees were breached, cut through in a crevasse through which the river scoured a new channel in its powerful and inexorable race to reach the Gulf. Eventually those channels would create their own natural levees. Some, perhaps most, of those channels that were violently created by a levee breaking would silt up at the point at which they began at the edge of the river, and the water in the channels flowed less frequently and with less volume. Thus were born the bayous of south Louisiana in general and in Jefferson Parish in particular. Subsequent floods from the Mississippi River slowly filled some of the bayous with silt; trees and other vegetation trapped more soil; and only the natural levees remained to show that water had once coursed near them. These are the natural high spots in Jefferson Parish.

During its millennia flowing through Jefferson, the Mississippi River has changed course several times. Like a fire hose reacting to the water pressure within it by twisting and turning if left alone, the river will shift its meandering course in response to the constriction of its flow by the banks and natural levees it has built up. About twenty-five hundred years ago, the river flowed almost due east from its current channel to a delta in what is now St. Bernard Parish. During that period Bayou des Familles on the Westbank and Bayou Metairie on the east bank were created. Hundreds of years later Bayou Barataria began as another channel distributing the river's flow toward the Gulf. The river would shift its main course to what is now Bayou Lafourche and then to the current channel through Plaquemines Parish before the arrival of Europeans. All these channels, large and small, left natural levees. Many of those levees have disappeared, and those that remain are the ridges along which human development took place. In the very low land of coastal Louisiana, even a few inches of elevation can be the difference between a location that can support the growth of trees and human habitation and one that cannot.

Human beings have always been attracted to high places. Children scare their parents by climbing up into trees. Big cities build tall buildings to display their wealth and power. Ancient civilizations in Central America and Egypt built tall pyramids to honor their deities and their dead. Medieval Europeans built great cathedrals that raised their roofs and spires toward God. Jefferson Parish has never had the building materials for raising elevated structures, so the first Jeffersonians, those people who probably arrived not long after the land was formed and trees took root, had to be creative and improvise with what was at hand. They found what they needed in clams.

For hundreds, even thousands, of years the people living in what is now the Westbank of Jefferson Parish gathered clams from the shallow, brackish lakes and bays that were readily accessible. The clams had a double purpose; they were food, however indigestible they may be to modern tastes, and the shells provided a building material to create high places in the pancake-flat terrain. These shell piles provided high land on which to camp when the river flooded and Gulf storms pushed water over the low land. The height of the shell piles, just as the size of buildings today, was an indication of prestige and status. Over generations, the shell piles grew and grew. When the Europeans arrived in the Barataria region, they found dozens of these shell mounds along the bayous. They even named one of the bayous for the shells, Bayou Coquille, the French word for "shell."

Having no wheeled vehicles and no draft animals, the Indians of the Barataria region likewise had no need for streets. They traveled by paths along the ridges and in dugout canoes along the bayous. The water courses were the streets. The Europeans saw the piles of clam shells and started helping themselves. They used the clam shells first to make lime and then for road construction, with no appreciation of the archaeological importance of what they were destroying.

To an archeologist an ancient pile of shells is a "midden," a word meaning "dunghill" or "junk heap," a prehistoric garbage dump. Such meaning did not deter someone from naming a street in the Oak Forest subdivision south of Estelle **Midden Drive.** Who would want to live on a street named for a garbage dump? It should be pointed out that the back of the subdivision is at the edge of Bayou des Familles, one of the bayous along which many middens were located, so the meaning of the word applies only to those nearby prehistoric sites. It is best to ignore the underlying meaning of the word.

Before a particularly large midden located at the northern limit of Barataria Bay was destroyed by removal of its shells, its high ground provided a place for Jean Lafitte and his compatriots to display and sell their smuggled goods, an open-air market called the Temple. Other middens, the high spots in the wetlands of the Barataria region, were similarly used.

Modern Jefferson Parish has erected high levees along the Mississippi River and for hurricane protection making them the highest land in the parish, just as the middens were for more than a thousand years earlier. Lacking true hills or even a contrived structure like Monkey Hill in New Orleans's Audubon Zoo, Jeffersonians have found high places in the names of some of its streets. There is a **Hill Street** in an industrial area of Old Jefferson. The only hill around there is a manmade structure a couple of blocks away, the embankment supporting the railroad tracks of the approach to the **Huey P. Long Bridge.** Other than the **Westbank Expressway,** the busiest street in Harvey is **Manhattan Boulevard.** Named for the principal borough and island of New York City, the namers of the Harvey street may not have realized that, in the language of the Lenape Indians who lived there, "Manhattan" (originally *Mannahatta*) means "Island of Many Hills." There's hardly a hill in Harvey, and certainly no natural ones, only some linear ones called levees.

On the east bank, Jefferson Parish is likewise bereft of hills and mountains, but there are streets that emphasize height. **Jefferson Heights Avenue** in Old Jefferson, **Colonial Heights Road** in River Ridge, and **Metairie Heights Avenue** in Old Metairie brought street naming to new heights. Anyone looking for high land in east Jefferson may believe they have found it on **Highland Avenue.** The street is squeezed into a section near the intersection of **Airline Drive** and **Clearview Parkway,** very close to those noisy, busy streets and the railroad tracks. Maybe the land on **Highland Avenue** is higher than surrounding property, maybe not. It may be reassuring to those who live there that their street intersects **Utopia Street.** On the other hand, the Garden of Memories graveyard is very close. Not far away, parallel to **Transcontinental Drive,** is **High Avenue.** If residents cannot *be* high on **High Avenue,** perhaps they can *get* high.

In Estelle there is a subdivision whose streets are named for some of the highest and most notable mountains in the world. The real-estate developers who created the subdivision liked to get high, literally. **Mt. Kennedy Drive** is named for a mountain in the St. Elias range in the Kluane National Park in Yukon, Canada, near the border with Alaska. The mountain is named for assassinated U.S. President John F. Kennedy. Nearby **Mt. Shasta Drive** gets its name from the mountain in California that is the site of ski resorts and is so beautiful that it is a symbol of and the brand name of a line of soft drinks. **Mt. Blanc Drive** is named for the highest mountain in Europe, in the Alps near where the borders of France, Switzerland, and Italy meet. Montblanc is also a brand name for elegant and expensive pens and watches. Can any readers name the presidents whose faces are carved in South Dakota's Mt. Rushmore? Maybe the residents of Estelle (Estellites? Estellese? Estellish?) who live on **Mt. Rushmore Drive** know the answer.

The Matterhorn of Switzerland is probably the most photographed mountain in the world. It pokes up into the sky like, well, the horn of some animal. Hundreds of climbers have died on its slopes and glaciers since modern mountain climbing began as a sport in the nineteenth century. The most difficult climb on **Mt. Matterhorn Drive** is getting up the steps of a house. The namesake of nearby **Mt. Whitney Drive** is in California, the highest point in the forty-eight contiguous states, only a relatively short distance from Death Valley, the lowest place in North America.

Even spelling-bee champions miss sometimes; so did those who named **Mt. Revarb Drive.** A search for a mountain with the name "Revarb" is a frustrating activity; there is no such place. Nevertheless, in the mountains of France there is a popular ski resort at a mountain with the name Mont Revard. One letter difference changes the name, and the street signs perpetuate the spelling error. Another ski resort is recognized in the name of **Mt. Arbois Court.** In the French Alps there is a ski area called Mont d'Arbois; the street namers made it easier for English speakers and readers. **Mt. Jura Court** is named for a range of mountains in Europe, parts of which are in France, Switzerland, and Germany.

Coming down from the heights of **Mt. Rushmore Drive,** a driver turns right onto **Barataria Boulevard** and in less than one block can get fancifully high again. A left turn onto improbably named **Hillcrest Drive** continues the fascination with heights. **Hillcrest Drive** goes up only in name; there is no hill, let alone a crest. The street actually goes down slightly from **Barataria Boulevard** as it crosses on a culvert over Bayou des Familles. Farther south in Estelle, connecting to **Leo Kerner-Lafitte Parkway,** is **Highland Meadows Drive,** the entrance to a residential development created out of the swamp—not even a high swamp.

Part of the attraction of living in Old Metairie is that much of the land is on the old Metairie Ridge, slightly higher than surrounding area, but "higher" is a relative term. In the alluvial geology of southeastern Louisiana, just a few inches of relative elevation can be the difference between getting wet and staying almost dry. In that spirit, there is a short street in Old Metairie that exaggerates the height of the ridge, **Crestmont Drive,** which means in literal terms "mountaintop." So, in the words of the old spiritual, when you are in Old Metairie, "Go tell it on the mountain," on **Crestmont Drive.**

Trivia answer: Mt. Rushmore bears the faces of Presidents George Washington, Thomas Jefferson, Abraham Lincoln, and Theodore Roosevelt.

Chapter 10
Harahan

James Harahan was the president of the Illinois Central Railroad in the early part of the twentieth century. The IC, as it was usually called, had a large marshal and maintenance yard in east Jefferson near its mainline tracks. There was a roundhouse to service the locomotives and turn them around. Many of the men who worked at that facility lived nearby. Also nearby was an experimental farm operated by Southern University. Either the experiments failed or they were so successful that there was no further need for an experimental farm, and Southern University put it up for sale. An investment group with James Harahan as its leader bought the farm in 1914 and developed it for residential living. During the same period, the Orleans-Kenner Line, a railroad that would more properly be called a streetcar line in twenty-first-century parlance, was opening up the land between New Orleans and Kenner for residential and agricultural use. The barn that housed the O-K Line cars was located just upriver from the S curve in the middle of Harahan, a facility that provided employment for workers who lived nearby. Every morning the first car would roll out of the barn at five and begin the long run between downtown New Orleans and the city limits of Kenner at the St. Charles Parish border. The last car left **Canal Street** in New Orleans at midnight.

Shortly after the O-K Line began operation, **Jefferson Highway** was built parallel to the streetcar-railroad tracks and provided another form of transportation as the automobile age began to grow by leaps. The O-K Line is memorialized by **O K Avenue** in Harahan, which connects to **Jefferson Highway** and the route of the old streetcar-railway, upriver from the site of the railway barn.

By 1924, the Harahan area had a sufficient population that it was incorporated as a municipality and named for the railroad man who had turned the experimental farm into a housing development. The town's first mayor was Frank Mayo. In fact, Harahan's second mayor was Frank Mayo, too, and he used a "Jr." after his name. Thus for several years Harahan's political leader was someone who could be called Mayor Mayo. (The mayors' name has nothing to do with what goes on the French bread in a po-boy sandwich.) The Mayos, *père et fils,* are remembered by the citizens of Harahan (Harahanians? Harahanish? Harahanites?) in a dedicated street, **Mayo Avenue.**

Long before the experimental farm that became Harahan was in business, there was big-time agriculture in the area. The Soniat Plantation occupied the land that became Colonial Country Club and its golf course, the most prominent landmark in Harahan. The plantation manor house was the first clubhouse of the country club, and the street alongside the club and the golf course is appropriately named **Colonial Club Drive.** The street begins at the end of the **River Road,** which in Harahan is named **Riverside Drive,** then goes toward Lake Pontchartrain, crosses **Jefferson Highway,** and ends at the Soniat Playground. The Soniat Plantation is remembered in the name of the playground, the Soniat Canal dividing Harahan from River Ridge, and **Soniat Avenue.** The site of the Soniat Plantation and Colonial Country Club is located on a point formed by long, meandering curve of the Mississippi River. To river travelers, the site is called Twelve Mile Point. Does any reader know what landmark on the river is twelve miles to or from Twelve Mile Point that gives it its name?

Harahan's **Riverside Drive** hugs the levee, but abruptly ends at Colonial Country Club. A motorist must proceed along **Colonial Club Drive** to **Jefferson Highway,** then turn left to continue an upriver journey. The **River Road** does not resume its up-against-the-levee route until **Jefferson Highway** ends at the eastern Kenner city limits, becomes **Reverend Richard Wilson Drive**, which then gets named **Third Street**, and reaches St. Charles Parish at the western Kenner city limits. There the **River Road** begins anew.

On a map, the lines marking the municipal limits of the city of Harahan give the city the shape of a skillet. The front edge of the "pan" part of the skillet is along the levee near **Hickory Avenue** upriver to just past **Normandy Avenue**, across **Jefferson Highway**, and along the drainage ditch next to **Folse Drive**, which is in River Ridge. The boundary goes north to where the ditch joins the Soniat Canal and then follows the canal to the railroad tracks. The "handle" of the Harahan skillet is a narrow strip of land on either side of **Hickory Avenue** between the Soniat Canal and the right of way for the high-voltage power lines. West of this strip of Harahan across the canal is River Ridge; east of the strip is Old Jefferson.

Hickory Avenue became an important roadway because the people of Harahan needed a link between **Jefferson Highway** and **Airline Highway**, later to become **Airline Drive**. In the early 1950s, the city of Harahan persuaded the state department of highways to make **Hickory Avenue** a paved state highway. That project increased the traffic between the two highways. There was a downside to this progress in transportation, though; the increasingly busy **Hickory Avenue** was only two lanes and crossed multiple sets of railroad tracks at a dangerous grade crossing. These tracks were part of the busiest railway access to New Orleans and its port; travel on **Hickory Avenue** was often delayed, sometimes for long periods, while locomotives shifted trains through nearby Mays Yard. There was much frustration, and occasionally fools and daredevils sped around the lowered warning gates in front of oncoming trains. Something needed to be done to provide safer, smoother, and less congested travel along **Hickory Avenue**.

Enter the highway planners, with a sense of humor and memories of childhood:

Hickory, dickory, dock,
The mouse ran up the clock.
The clock struck one,
The mouse ran down,
Hickory, dickory, dock.

And so it came to pass that, in their wisdom and foresight, the highway planners decided that the best way to ease the congestion and improve safety was to construct a bypass road parallel to **Hickory Avenue** with an overpass over the railroad tracks. Not only did the new bypass road do what it was designed to do, it also spurred development and construction. Because it was a partner to older **Hickory Avenue**, the new roadway was named **Dickory Avenue**. The planners didn't stop there; they named one of the streets connecting **Hickory** and **Dickory**—what else—**Dock Street**. Not to be left out of the fun, the people in the Jefferson Parish traffic-engineering department, located on **Dickory Avenue**, named the driveway into their facility **Mouse Lane** and attached a sketch of a clock and a mouse to the fence next to the stanchion holding the street signs. Who said bureaucrats can't have a good time at work?

Some day in the distant future **Dickory Avenue** will continue south all the way to **Jefferson Highway.** Until then southbound traffic must exit left at **Mounes Street** through the industrial area of Elmwood or turn right at **Gardner Street** to **Hickory Avenue** in order to reach **Jefferson Highway** and **River Road/Riverside Drive**.

Along most of its length **Dickory Avenue** is right up to the city limits of Harahan, meaning that the street is officially in unincorporated Old Jefferson. There is much confusion in some of the names of businesses along the busy roadway. The Harahan skillet "handle" is so narrow that someone can stand in River Ridge at the edge of the

Soniat Canal and with a strong swing of a bat knock a ball
completely across Harahan and into Old Jefferson. Perhaps
merchants like the name "River Ridge"—it has a good
rhythm—better than either "Harahan," "Old Jefferson,"
or even "Elmwood," because a large apartment complex
with an entrance on the east side of **Dickory Avenue** and
situated completely in Old Jefferson calls itself the Creeks
of River Ridge. Not only is the development not in River
Ridge, but there are no creeks, not even a bayou. Across
Dickory Avenue from the Creeks, between **Dickory** and
Hickory avenues and facing the short connection named
Dufrene Street, is a retail establishment called the Cellars
of River Ridge. This wine shop and delicatessen is within
the narrow Harahan city limits; River Ridge is a couple of
blocks away across the Soniat Canal, and there's nary a
cellar under the store. Nevertheless, these names fit well
in a commercial neighborhood that takes its name from a
nursery rhyme.

Can any readers remember another verse following
"Hickory, Dickory, Dock. . ." and the mouse?

Trivia answers: Twelve Mile Point is located twelve river
miles from Jackson Square.

The second verse of "Hickory, Dickory, Dock" goes as
follows:

Hickory, dickory, dock
The bird looked at the clock.
The clock struck two,
Away she flew,
Hickory, dickory, dock.

Hickory Avenue and Mouse Lane are one block away.

Chapter 11
We Go West and Westwego

On the Westbank of Jefferson Parish, west of Gretna, are Harvey, Marrero, Westwego, Nine Mile Point, Bridge City, Avondale, and Waggaman. Before getting into a further discussion of the streets of some of these communities, an explanation of the loose use of the word "west" and the term "Westbank" is appropriate. References to the west side of the Mississippi River, more accurately called the right descending bank, are in the uppercase combined word "Westbank," but the opposite side of the river is called the "east bank." There's a reason for this usage.

Before the **Crescent City Connection** bridge and the **Westbank Expressway** were built, the west side of the river opposite New Orleans, from Algiers upriver to the **Huey P. Long Bridge,** was called, in the diction-mangling idiom that is part of New Orleans culture, "over the river." For many years the *Times-Picayune* had a separate classified section for advertisers on the west side that was called "Over the River." There was a connotation of social class in that usage, with the semirural and blue-collar industrial communities on the Westbank sneered at to some degree by the educated and white-collar people of the city. The term "Westbank" began as a term of pride, often spoken in the same breath with its description by inhabitants as the "best bank." "Westbank" became a proper name, capitalized with pride, and with no equivalent on the east bank.

Still, to call one bank "east" and the other "west" requires a flexible sense of geography. A quick look at a map shows that at no point in its course from the St. Charles Parish line at Kenner to the Orleans Parish line at **Monticello Avenue** does the Mississippi River flow directly south, creating accurately described east and west banks. In general, the river flows mostly from west to east, with turns around Twelve Mile Point, Nine Mile Point, and the beginning of the great meander that forms the crescent of the city of New Orleans. If the compass directions are strictly used, the Westbank is, for the most part, south of the east bank.

Immediately westward, by the compass, from Gretna is Harvey. For many in the New Orleans metropolitan area, the name "Harvey" is merely the first part of "Harvey Canal," the two words rarely being separated. Indeed, the Harvey Canal could be considered the main street of that community and its reason for existence. Before there were locks in the levee allowing boats to move to and from the canal and the Mississippi River, Captain Joseph Harvey created a railway that towed boats onto a submerged carriage, then hauled them up and over the levee. The original canal was called the "d'Estrehan Ditch" after Jean Baptiste d'Estrehan, the landowner who used German immigrants to dig it in 1724. The canal was an important transportation link in the days before railroads, automobiles, and good roads. It connected the Mississippi River to Bayou Barataria and the waters to the south. The d'Estrehan heritage of the canal is kept alive in the name of the street that parallels the Harvey Canal on the west side, **Destrehan Avenue.**

Captain Harvey expanded the canal, and commerce through and along it thrived. A lock was built in 1907, removing the need to move boats up and over the levee. This device was a primitive lock, and it was no more than a gate between the river and the canal. It could be used only when the water levels on each side were approximately the same. A full lock that could move vessels between the river and the canal was built in the early 1920s when the federal government took over the canal and made it part of the Gulf Intracoastal Waterway System then under construction.

The Harvey Canal's importance as a location for

shipbuilding and marine repairs is reflected in the name of a nearby street, **Clydesbank Drive.** Located in Scotland along the River Clyde, Clydesbank or Clydebank is the heart of shipbuilding and repair in the United Kingdom. The Scottish theme is continued in Harvey in the names of **Angus Drive, Aberdeen Drive, Argyll Street, Glasgow Drive,** and **Lochlomand Drive.** These are all places or cities in Scotland. In Scotland, the largest inland lake is Loch Lomond. Misspellings in Jefferson Parish street names are not unusual, and nobody has been known to get lost because a street name messed up a letter or two. There is a **Scottsdale Drive,** too, to emphasize the Scottish theme.

The television series *Star Trek* began with a voice-over solemnly announcing, "Space: the final frontier." Interest in America's space program is shown by the names of the streets in the Woodlawn Park neighborhood. **North Von Braun Court** and **South Von Braun Court** remember the name of Wernher von Braun, a German rocket scientist who worked for the Nazis in World War II and then created the space program for the United States. Space-exploration projects get streets named for them, too: **Apollo Avenue** and **Gemini Street. Titan Street, Centaur Street,** and **Saturn Street** commemorate the names of the rockets used to send astronauts and satellites into space. The name of **Jupiter Street** comes from a rocket of the same name used to propel ballistic missiles. **Vulcan Street** is named for a rocket built by the Russians. There are **Telstar Street,** named for the first orbiting satellite put into space by the United States, and **Orbit Court** as well. Maybe Harvey and the Westbank are the final frontier.

Moving west from Harvey requires crossing the Harvey Canal. Before the **Westbank Expressway** was built, the only way across the canal was by bridges that opened and closed. The traffic in the canal and the traffic on the roads both increased, and there were long lines of motorists, patient and otherwise, often waiting for the bridges to reopen. Before the elevated expressway was constructed, the **Harvey Tunnel** provided passage under the canal and under the boats that would have kept the drawbridges in the up position. When the **Westbank Expressway** was completed as a limited-access highway, the canal traffic was no longer a concern to vehicular traffic. A high-level bridge moves the traffic over the canal, although those who prefer to stay grounded can still drive under the canal through the tunnel.

Coming down from the bridge over or out of the tunnel under the Harvey Canal, the next community westward is Marrero. It is discussed in Chapter 8.

Upriver and west from Marrero is the only city in the United States whose name is a complete sentence, Westwego. The city's name comes from a railroad yard that acquired the term as a slogan in the nineteenth century. The nearby residential neighborhood was known as Salaville, after Pablo Sala, a merchant and landowner.

Many Westwegans (Westwegish?) are descendents of refugees from the deadliest storm ever to hit Jefferson Parish. On October 1, 1893, before the existence of the National Hurricane Center, radar, or any scientific method of predicting the strength and path of a hurricane, a killer storm struck Grand Isle and the neighboring community of Chênière Caminada. More than sixteen hundred people were killed. The entire fishing and farming community of Chênière Caminada was destroyed, and 822 people were killed there alone. Refugees fled for days through the marsh and swamps and eventually reached Salaville, a new development along the Westbank just downriver from Nine Mile Point. Pablo Sala had acquired and subdivided land along a canal from the Mississippi River to Lake Catouatchie. The canal allowed commerce across Lake Salvador from Bayou Lafourche to be transported to the markets in New Orleans. The canal was variously called the Barataria Canal, the Company Canal, and the Westwego Canal. Like the Harvey Canal, the canal alongside which Sala established his community was the main street of the community. Sala was not a resident of Salaville, but he reduced the price of his lots for the refugees from Chênière Caminada, who created a mild population boom along the canal.

The Westwego Canal was eventually closed and filled; the competition from the Harvey Canal and the expanding railroad system doomed it as a commercial enterprise. The booming railroad yard became known as Westwego, a slogan used by the railroad workers, and the name spread to include the surrounding residential and agricultural areas. Salaville merged into the village of Westwego when it was incorporated in 1919. The community of Salaville and Pablo Sala are not forgotten, however. They are memorialized in **Sala Avenue,** in the same location paralleling the long-gone Westwego Canal.

Jeffersonians should be glad that an ambitious canal project, vigorously advocated for several decades by business and political leaders, never happened. The U.S. Army Corps of Engineers was urged to construct a deep-water canal at the approximate location of the old Westwego Canal, but was to be much deeper and wider. Its route was a shortcut for seagoing vessels in the Mississippi River and went south through Bayou Segnette, Lake Catouatchie, and Lake Salvador, then through Barataria Bay and into the open Gulf of Mexico through Barataria Pass between Grand Isle and Grande Terre. Much to the disappointment of the movers and shakers who wanted the channel built, with its resulting service roads and commercial development, the corps chose a route through eastern New Orleans and St. Bernard Parish. They called the channel the Mississippi River Gulf Outlet (MRGO), and it proved to be a disaster maker, channeling the storm surges from Hurricane Betsy in 1965 and Hurricane Katrina in 2005 that devastated St. Bernard Parish and eastern New Orleans. It was also an environmental disaster because the banks of the channel kept washing away, eventually making the MRGO three times wider than it had been constructed. Had that channel been dug through Jefferson Parish, much of the Westbank would have suffered the same fate as lower St. Bernard.

Bayou Segnette, Bayou Segnette State Park, and **Segnette Boulevard** get their names from an early French landowner, Jean-Baptiste Senet. He was the son of Louis Senet, the first captain of the port of New Orleans in the 1720s. The French name "Senet" is of the same etymological origin as the English word "senate," the Latin term for "wise one." Monsieur Senet and his son Jean-Baptiste Senet were owners of a large tract of land in the eighteenth century in what is now Westwego. The bayou was at the rear of the property, and somehow the spelling went from "senet" to "segnette." In those days consistent, regular spelling was not particularly important, in either French or English. After the Senet family name ceased to be associated with the area, the "Segnette" spelling became permanent. Today **Segnette Boulevard** connects the **Westbank Expressway** with **Lapalco Boulevard** and sets the western border of Bayou Segnette State Park.

Proceeding westward ("West we go!") from Westwego on **Fourth Street,** which is also **Louisiana Highway 18,** a driver passes the whimsically named streets of Nine Mile Point, crosses **U.S. Highway 90,** and goes through Bridge City, the site of the Fairfield Plantation, near the giant Avondale shipyard. The road goes around the shipyard and the railroad yard and becomes the **River Road.**

Next is the community of Waggaman, named for George Augustus Waggaman, who established the Avondale Plantation in 1840. A series of streets in Waggaman are named for places and institutions in the District of Columbia, starting with **District Drive.** There are **Federal Drive, Judiciary Drive, Treasury Drive, Dome Drive, Cabinet Drive, Council Drive, Rotunda Drive,** and **Delegate Drive.** The official guest house for important visitors to Washington is Blair House. **Blair Drive** is one of Waggaman's streets as well. **Georgetown Drive** gets its name from the section of Washington by that name. **Congress Drive** and

Senate Drive are there, too. Unlike the First Amendment of the U.S. Constitution, there is no separation of church and state in the streets of Waggaman. Side-by-side and crossing the streets named for places and institutions in the nation's capitol are **Priest Street, Bishop Drive, Mission Court, Chapel Lane, Church Street** and **Cathedral Drive.** Bordering the subdivision on the west is appropriately named **Capitol Drive.** Salute the flag with one hand and finger a rosary with the other.

Chapter 12

Hail to the Chiefs

Naming streets for presidents is usually not controversial. Most of the presidents of the United States are dead. Several are universally considered to be heroes of the country; some are obscure and are noncontroversial because they have not left much in terms of historic or social legacy. Jefferson Parish, like many communities throughout the United States, has many streets named for the men who have led the country since George Washington first took office in 1789. The father of our country is named on **Washington Avenue** in Harvey and on **Washington Street** in Kenner.

In Gretna, there are streets named for the first five presidents, in chronological order beginning at the Mississippi River with **Washington Street**. Next is, of course, **Adams Street** for John Adams. The parish's namesake is next on **Jefferson Street**. Thomas Jefferson has several streets honoring him in the parish that bears his name beginning with **Jefferson Highway**. **Jefferson Street**, **Jefferson Park Avenue**, and **Jefferson Heights Avenue** are in Old Jefferson, and **Jefferson Avenue** is in Old Metairie. There is also a **Jefferson Avenue** on Grand Isle.

President James Madison, often called the father of the Constitution, follows Thomas Jefferson in Gretna on **Madison Street**. Madison was president at the time of the Battle of New Orleans, January 8, 1815, and issued a pardon for Jefferson Parish's most famous criminal, Jean Lafitte, for his service to the United States in that battle. Jefferson Parish had not yet been established at the time of the battle or the pardon, but Lafitte and his henchmen had their headquarters on Grand Isle and Grande Terre, which eventually became part of the parish.

Monroe Street is the next in the Gretna series. James Monroe is the president who formulated the Monroe Doctrine, which aimed to halt further European colonization in the Western Hemisphere.

There is no separate street named for the sixth president, John Quincy Adams, so he can be remembered on the street named for his father, the second president. There is, however, a **Quincy Street** in Metairie, the Q in the alphabetical series of street names there.

The hero of the Battle of New Orleans, Andrew Jackson, became the seventh president of the United States. He is remembered in Kenner on **Jackson Street** and in Westwego on another **Jackson Street.**

Andrew Jackson was succeeded by New Yorker Martin Van Buren. He gets a street in Metairie in his name, **Van Buren Avenue.** Following President Van Buren was the man who served for less than one month, William Henry Harrison. He caught a cold during the inauguration, which developed into pneumonia and killed him. Despite the fact that he had no time to establish a presidential legacy, there is a **Harrison Avenue** in Metairie, an interrupted westward extension of the street of the same name in the Lakeview neighborhood of New Orleans. Whether the street is named specifically for the shortest-serving president is not significant; the street bears his name anyway.

There is a **Tyler Avenue** in Harahan, but it is not clear that it was named for the tenth U.S. president, John Tyler. In an interesting coincidence, **Tyler Avenue** intersects **Lincoln Avenue** and is near **Grover Avenue, Calvin Avenue,** and **Franklin Avenue.** There are no presidents with surnames Grover, Calvin, and Franklin, but Grover Cleveland served twice as president but not by reelection, the only president to do so. Cleveland was the twenty-second and the twenty-fourth president of the United States. There are **Cleveland**

Court and **Cleveland Place** in Metairie, but they were not named for this president.

Franklin Pierce, the fourteenth president, is not represented in any Jefferson Parish street unless, and it is far from clear for whom it was named, **Franklin Avenue** in Harahan was named for this little-known president. **Franklin Avenue** in Gretna is named for Benjamin Franklin.

Jefferson Parish has no street named for the eleventh president, James Knox Polk, but President Zachary Taylor, Polk's successor, is the named president of **Taylor Street**, parallel to and one block away from **Jackson Street** in Kenner.

President Taylor did not live out his term. On July 9, 1850, Millard Fillmore went from being vice president to the thirteenth president. Number thirteen was unlucky for him. He was the last member of the Whig political party to become president, but he was so inadequate at the job that his own party did not nominate him for reelection in 1852. Not discouraged, Fillmore ran for the presidency as the candidate of the Know-Nothing Party and lost. Despite his undistinguished presidency, Millard Fillmore is remembered by a street in Kenner, **Filmore Street**. Perhaps it is fitting that the president who spelled his names with two *L*s in each and is remembered mostly for his mediocrity has his name misspelled, with a single *L* on the street named for him.

After Millard Fillmore and his forgettable presidency, the next two presidents, Franklin Pierce and James Buchanan, were forgotten when names for Jefferson Parish streets were being selected. But Buchanan was followed by the president who achieved greatness in leading the nation through the worst crisis in its history.

The sixteenth president, Abraham Lincoln, has three streets named for him. **Lincoln Avenue** and **Lincolnshire Drive** are in Marrero, and another **Lincoln Avenue** can be found in Harahan. After President Lincoln, there was little interest in naming streets for Andrew Johnson, number seventeen; Ulysses S. Grant, number eighteen; Rutherford B. Hayes, number nineteen; or assassinated President James Garfield. In fact, no president after Lincoln until number twenty-five, William McKinley, has his name on any Jefferson Parish street.

William McKinley, the third president to be assassinated, is remembered by **McKinley Street** in Kenner in a subdivision whose streets are named for national parks. Mount McKinley in Alaska is the highest mountain in North America, and at the time the street was named, it was the name of the national park in which the mountain is located. The name of the park was later changed to Denali National Park and Preserve, the local name for the mountain, but the big mountain still bears President McKinley's name.

Upon President McKinley's death, his vice president, Theodore Roosevelt, became, at age forty-two, the youngest president in history. He was energetic and opinionated, leading America into an era of international expansion. He established the first national parks and sent the U.S. Navy's Great White Fleet around the world in a show of the flag. In Kenner, in a group of streets named for some of the states of the union, there is **Roosevelt Boulevard.** It may be named for the twenty-sixth president, but is more likely a memorial to his cousin, the thirty-second president, Franklin D. Roosevelt.

Theodore Roosevelt, the youngest president was succeeded in office by William H. Taft, the largest president. President Taft was also the last president who was a member of the Unitarian Church. He did not much care for being president and was not reelected. He was a law professor when President Warren G. Harding nominated him to be the chief justice of the U.S. Supreme Court, a job he relished. He wrote, "I don't remember that I ever was president." Those who live on **Taft Park** in Kenner can remember him, even if the street is not actually named for him.

Wilson is such a common surname that it cannot be said with certainty that **Wilson Street** in Metairie was named for the twenty-eighth president, Woodrow Wilson, an intellectual who led the United States through World War I. He was succeeded by Warren G. Harding, whose presidency was marked by rumors and accusations of insider dealings and corruption. Harding died of a heart attack while in office and was succeeded by Calvin Coolidge. Political journalist Walter Lippmann wrote that Coolidge's political genius was his ability to do nothing effectively. Despite their less-than-inspiring presidencies, both Presidents Harding and Coolidge are named on streets in the Rio Vista neighborhood of Old Jefferson, **Harding Street** and **Coolidge Street**. Perhaps they were so honored simply because they were the presidents at the time that neighborhood was being developed. As mentioned previously, there is a **Calvin Avenue** in Harahan, but its connection with President Coolidge is only inferential.

The next president in chronological order named on a Jefferson Parish street is Dwight D. Eisenhower, who is discussed in Chapter 3 and for whom **Eisenhower Avenue** in Metairie is named.

The Kennedy Heights subdivision in the Avondale-Waggaman section of the Westbank was named for President John F. Kennedy, but there is no street there named for him. **Kennedy Drive** in Gretna was most likely named before the thirty-fifth president was assassinated on November 22, 1963, and on the Metairie lakefront, **Kennedy Street** also predates President Kennedy. However, **Mt. Kennedy Drive** in Estelle gets its name from the mountain named for President Kennedy.

Readers will look in vain for any Jefferson Parish street named for a president after John F. Kennedy. How would Jeffersonians like the idea of a "Nixon Lane" or a "Carter Court"?

Chapter 13

Metairie

Sometimes Metairie gets pronounced with only two syllables and comes out "Metry." However it is pronounced, **Metairie Road** is one of the oldest and most important streets in Jefferson Parish. From its humble beginning as a dirt trail to reach the small farms along the Metairie Ridge, the relatively high land left thousands of years ago when Bayou Metairie was a distributary channel of the Mississippi River, flowing and overflowing with silt-filled water, to its current status as one of the most desirable neighborhoods in the New Orleans metropolitan area, Old Metairie is synonymous with fine homes and the good life of which Jefferson Parish is so proud. There is little sign left of Bayou Metairie, only the depression in the earth on which the westbound lanes of **Metairie Road** are built next to Metairie Cemetery in Orleans Parish. The part of the lagoon where **City Park Avenue** meets **North Carrollton Avenue** at the front of City Park is also a vestige of Bayou Metairie.

The development of Metairie produced streets with names from the families of the developers and some of their interests. Wealthy French pharmacist and investor Henri Bonnabel bought land along Bayou Metairie and established a plantation. Henri's son, Alfred Bonnabel, was one of the leaders of Jefferson Parish for several decades. Alfred served forty-five years on the Jefferson Parish School Board and twenty-five years on the police jury, the predecessor to the Jefferson Parish Council. Alfred's wife was Laura Brockenbraugh Rappelye, and one of their grandchildren was named Elmeer. (Who'd want to name their child "Elmeer"?) From this family, Metairie received the street names **Bonnabel Boulevard, Brockenbraugh Street, Brockenbraugh Court,** and **Elmeer Avenue.** The Bonnabel family's home was located on a street they named, appropriately, **Homestead Avenue.**

In the third generation of the Bonnabel family, Alfred E., son of Alfred, was married to a lady named Luellen who had an interest in classical mythology. As the Bonnabels prospered and developed more streets and subdivisions, Luellen Bonnabel put her touch to the street-naming business. On the east side of the development she named **Phosphor Avenue,** a name from classical Greek meaning "light bearer" and designating the morning star that rises in the east. Consistent with that name, Luellen made the last street in the development to the west **Hesper Street,** symbolizing the evening star that appears in the west at twilight.

Other mythological names abound in Metairie, thanks to Mrs. Bonnabel. **Aurora Avenue** is from the Latin word for "dawn" and the goddess of first light. Parallel to that street is **Orion Avenue,** named for the mythological hunter who twinkles high above as one of the most easily identified constellations in the night sky.

The sun god of the ancient Greeks was Helios, who gives his name to the element helium because scientists first observed it on the sun before it was discovered on Earth. The sun god gets a street named for him in Luellen Bonnabel's Metairie, **Helios Avenue,** but it doesn't get pronounced the way she intended. As written in English, spoken phonetically, and close to the Greek pronunciation, "Helios" should sound *HEE-LEE-OS.* Mrs. Bonnabel was not expecting New Orleans street-name pronunciation to be exported to her beautiful and elegant Metairie with its classical names of streets. In New Orleans, the streets named for the Greek muses of antiquity have for generations had their pronunciations mangled. **Terpsichore Street,** if spoken close to the Greek origin, is pronounced **Terp-SIC-o-ree**. New Orleans speakers call it *TERP-see-coar*. One wonders if the muse of dance would know when her name was called. **Melpomene Street,** which should be *MEL-POM-o-nee*, became **MEL-po-MEEN**. This practice of mispronouncing classical Greek names moved into Metairie, and with a little dyslexia that transposed the *i* and *o* in "Helios," the street's name gets pronounced *Heh-LOYCE*. It's still spelled **Helios Avenue,** and a few purists pronounce it in the correct way.

This brings up the question: What does one call the inhabitants of Metairie? In his fascinating history of Metairie, *Metairie: A Tongue of Land to Pasture,* Monsignor Henry Bezou, for many years the pastor of St. Francis Xavier Parish on **Metairie Road,** calls his parishioners and their neighbors "Metairieites." Could they not be Metairish, Metairese, or Metairians? They could even be called Metronians, which makes them sound like a group from some planet discovered by Mr. Spock of *Star Trek.* Monsignor Bezou's usage has been in place for many years, so Metairie inhabitants will have to be Metairieites.

Other classical Greek street names are on **Homer Street, Hesiod Street,** and **Demosthenes Street.** Homer, the best known of the ancient classical writers, was the author of *The Iliad* and *The Odyssey.* Hesiod was a poet of ancient Greece. Demosthenes was the most famous orator of classical Greece, a statesman who lived in the fourth century BC.

Two Roman goddesses are honored on **Pomona Street** and **Feronia Street,** parallel and one block apart. Pomona was the goddess of fruit trees and orchards; Feronia was an obscure ancient deity, predating the Romans, a goddess of fertility and liberty. It was said that she was worshipped by slaves.

In *The Odyssey,* Homer tells the story of the Sirens, the female entities whose enticing songs lured sailors to their deaths when their ships crashed on rocks as the sailors were trying to reach the singers. There is a **Siren Street** in Metairie near the end of **Bonnabel Boulevard,** a place where sailors launch their boats into Lake Pontchartrain and bring them back. A siren is also the name of an ugly, slimy amphibian that looks a lot like an eel and lives in the mud of swamps in Jefferson Parish. **Siren Street** is obviously not named to honor this slippery creature. In keeping with the theme of classical mythology, it is apparent that **Siren Street** was named for Homer's deadly ladies. It may therefore be a good idea for boaters at the Bonnabel Boat Launch not to listen to music originating from **Siren Street.**

Two Roman emperors get Metairie streets named for them, **Nero Street** and **Claudius Street.** Nero is famous—or infamous—for playing the fiddle while the city of Rome burned. Emperor Claudius was the uncle of the emperor who immediately preceded him, the madman Caligula. Claudius adopted his fourth wife's son, Nero, and made him his successor as emperor.

Until 1909, there was no public road-building program in Jefferson Parish. **Metairie Road** was a dirt track full of mud holes, impassable in rainy weather. In 1910 the state highway department was created, and the roads-and-streets program improved **Metairie Road,** grading it for better drainage. Development of Metairie got a boost when a streetcar line along **Metairie Road** was built in 1913, carrying passengers from the end of **Canal Street** in Orleans Parish to **Shrewsbury Road.** Paving of the major Jefferson Parish roads came in the 1920s, with **Shrewsbury Road** from **Metairie Road** to **Jefferson Highway** completed, as well as all of **Metairie Road.**

In the early twentieth century, George C. Friedrichs was a real-estate developer in Metairie. He also owned a horse-racing track from 1903 to 1907. He is remembered on **Friedrichs Avenue,** a street that intersects **Metairie Road** near the Orleans Parish line.

In the nineteenth century, the Betz family, emigrants from Germany looking for fortune and new beginnings in Metairie, acquired land and left their name on **Betz Place.**

Bettors have no place to place bets on Betz Place in Old Metairie.

The name shows up in Old Jefferson as well; **Betz Avenue** near Ochsner Medical Center runs from the **River Road** to the railroad tracks. One member of the Betz family, Valentine Betz, served as a Jefferson Parish police juror from 1896 to 1915.

Around the same time that the Betz brothers were acquiring land in Metairie, Frank Fagot operated a grocery store on **Metairie Road** near **Bonnabel Boulevard.** He was a business and social leader of the day. Today **Fagot Avenue** is pronounced *FAG-gott* and elicits sneers and snickers. The original French pronunciation is *FAH-GO,* and the name comes from the French word meaning a bundle of sticks used for firewood. In British English usage, "faggot" is used with the same meaning. In both French and English there are many slang meanings, not all polite. For example, British slang uses "fag" to mean cigarette, appropriate to its underlying meaning of a firewood stick. Metairieites who live on **Fagot Avenue** must get weary of explaining the origin of the name of their street and its pronunciation.

Residents of San Francisco generally don't like to hear the city called "Frisco." The same can be said for New Orleanians who hear their city called "New Er-leens." Nevertheless, there is a **Frisco Avenue** in Metairie. Its close parallel proximity to the railroad tracks that cross **Metairie Road** is revealing. As drivers sit and wait for trains that seem to move no faster than a furlong per fortnight, they might consider that there was once a railroad company called the Frisco Line or simply the Frisco. On September 1, 1909, the Frisco Line began service to New Orleans.

One hundred years ago and more there were many, many railroads, some with long and rhythmic names. The Frisco Line was the operational name of the St. Louis-San Francisco Railway Company. The name "Frisco" was started and used by employees and customers far from the city of San Francisco; the railroad never made it to the California city. Other names from the golden years of railroads included the Yazoo & Mississippi Valley Railroad Company and the Gulf, Mobile & Ohio, both of which had service to New Orleans. The Frisco operated its trains in New Orleans on tracks owned by the Yazoo & Mississippi Valley Railroad Company. By coincidence, there is a street in Arabi in St. Bernard Parish named **Friscoville Avenue** and is historically associated with the railroad in that parish.

Nursery Avenue is named for a nursery, but not the kind where young children are raised. Rather, the nursery was a place where Harry Papworth raised plants for sale. Horticulturist Papworth established a large nursery along **Metairie Road** beginning in 1901. Although the nursery operation is long gone, a record of that history remains in the name of **Papworth Avenue** and the Metairie streets named for his flowers: **Dahlia Street, Violet Street, Rose Street,** and **Pink Street.** There is a **Narcissus Street** among all the other flowers, but Monsignor Bezou wrote that it was named for Narcisse Lassé, an early Metairie landowner.

Fans of Elvis Presley will be disappointed to know that
Elvis Court, which connects to **Metairie Road,** is not named
for the King. Elvis was born on January 8, 1935, and **Elvis
Court** was already in existence at that time. The street and
its name were the products of the Elvis Realty Company,
with no relation or connection to the singer and performer
from Tupelo, Mississippi. Thank ya ver' much. Elvis has left
the building.

The western end of **Metairie Road** is its intersection
with **Airline Drive, Shrewsbury Road,** and **Severn Avenue.**
Shrewsbury Road, nearby **Labarre Road,** and **Metairie
Road** were once the only transportation grid in east
Jefferson, making a connection to the **River Road.** In 1935
Airline Highway was completed, but the man who made it
happen, Huey Long, was assassinated before he could fulfill
his dream of driving from Baton Rouge to New Orleans
on a more or less straight road. The commercial airline
industry was getting a good start in 1935, and the straight
line between New Orleans and Baton Rouge was similar to
the route an airplane would take. It was a much quicker
automobile trip than the winding curves of **Jefferson
Highway-River Road** along the levee.

The name **Severn Avenue** fits well as an extension
of **Shrewsbury Road.** The Severn River is the longest in
England, just as the Mississippi is the longest in the United
States. And just as the Mississippi River makes a large
loop around New Orleans, the Severn River makes a loop
around the city of Shrewsbury in England. Or it is more
geographically correct to say that each city was established
in a loop of a river, the loops coming before the cities.

In the northeast corner of Jefferson Parish is a community
that, by postal address, is part of Metairie, but most residents
know it as Bucktown. There are several stories of varying
degrees of veracity to account for the name, but the principal
one is that it was named for a local hunter, fisherman, and
raconteur named Buck Worley. There were hunting and
fishing camps in the area as well as a commercial fishing

fleet for catching shrimp and crabs. Worley shot a buck and hung its horns on the rail of a bridge over the 17th Street Canal, and thereafter the neighborhood became known as Bucktown. Bucktown was devastated by Hurricane Katrina, and new levees and a new pumping station were built on the canal.

Bucktown remains connected to Orleans Parish by a roadway that begins on the New Orleans side of the canal as the **New Orleans-Hammond Highway.** Across the bridge in Bucktown, the street becomes the **Metairie-Hammond Highway** and ends abruptly a few blocks west at **Chickasaw Avenue.** This road is the remnant of a highway that never was.

When automobiles were becoming numerous and popular in the 1920s, there was a project to build a road from New Orleans westward along the south shore of Lake Pontchartrain, then north along the western shoreline, across Pass Manchac and north into Tangipahoa Parish, ending at the city of Hammond. The knowledge and expertise for building roads through marshes was, to say the least, not yet well developed, and the planners naively thought that all they needed to do was erect a six-foot levee and put a road on top of it. Immediately portions began to crumble and erode. It was never opened completely along its entire length. The construction of the Bonnet Carré Spillway in the 1930s eliminated the road at the Lake Pontchartrain side of the flood-control structure. The severe hurricane of 1947 tore up much of what was left in Jefferson Parish of the **New Orleans-Hammond Highway,** and some of its remnants became a walking and bicycle path. Then Hurricane Katrina and subsequent levee reconstruction all but obliterated what once was a grand idea. Less than a mile is left from its beginning at **Pontchartrain Boulevard** in New Orleans to its end at **Chickasaw Avenue.**

On the official Web site the twenty-four-mile-long elevated roadway across Lake Pontchartrain is identified as the **Lake Pontchartrain Causeway Bridge.** Most people

call it simply the **Causeway**. The name is a redundancy.
The word "causeway" is a generic term for a type of bridge,
one that is elevated over water or wet ground. Using the
double phrase "causeway bridge" is the same as the usage
"Esplanade Avenue." (An esplanade *is* an avenue.) This
observation is pedantic to be sure, but calling the **Causeway**
"the causeway bridge" is right up there with ATM machine
and PIN number. Whatever the usage, however, the **Lake
Pontchartrain Causeway** is one of the most significant
roads in Jefferson Parish.

When the **Causeway** opened in 1956, Metairie consisted
mostly of what is now called Old Metairie and some
businesses and residential subdivisions along **Airline
Highway. Veterans Memorial Highway** was under
construction, but planners could see that the extension
of **Harlem Avenue** toward Lake Pontchartrain, linking it
to the new causeway and changing its name to **Causeway
Boulevard,** would create an economic boom for east
Jefferson. They were right. The intersection of **Causeway
Boulevard** and **Veterans Memorial Boulevard** became and
remains one of the busiest in the metropolitan area, one of
the most desired commercial locations, with proximity to
the interchange (forever under construction) at **Interstate
10** and **Causeway Boulevard.**

As busy and important as the **Causeway** is, linking
Jefferson Parish with commuter-filled St. Tammany Parish,
it has always had that bland, colorless name. It took several
years for the **Greater New Orleans Bridge** crossing the
Mississippi River to get the name of the **Crescent City
Connection,** and the **Huey P. Long Bridge** has always had
that name. The **Causeway** is just the **Causeway.** There
are probably many politicians on both sides of the lake,
dead and not quite, who are dying to have the **Causeway**
named for them. But they should restrain their egos lest
they get something else named for them. The following is
an example of why politicians should not wish for public
projects to be named for them.

In 2008 in San Francisco, the city to which the St. Louis-San Francisco Railway Company never made it, a proposal did make it on to the ballot to rename the Oceanside Wastewater Treatment Facility the George W. Bush Sewage Plant. The proponents were, to say the least, not fans of President Bush. The voters of San Francisco turned down the proposition, not out of respect for the outgoing president, but because the name change would have cost several thousand dollars. So politicians should be wary of getting an old bridge named after them; they may live to see headlines saying something like "John Smith Bridge falls into lake" or "Jane Smith Causeway collapses." The names **Lake Pontchartrain Causeway** and the **Causeway** will probably never be changed. And for many it will always be "the causeway bridge" even as they draw money from an ATM machine using their PIN numbers.

Crossing **Causeway Boulevard** not far from the south end of the **Causeway** is **Melvil Dewey Drive.** The headquarters of the Jefferson Parish Library was once at that corner, and the street was named after the man who invented the Dewey Decimal System, the alpha-numerical system for cataloging library books. Melvil Dewey was a strong advocate of phonetic spelling in English, forming the Spelling Reform Association. His name was originally Melville Dewey, but he changed it to Melvil Dui to eliminate unnecessary letters. But the "Dui" part didn't stick.

Two adjacent Metairie streets offer a study in the origin of names, in both cases hundreds of years old. The two parallel streets, one block apart, are named for regions in foreign countries, although that was probably not what the developers had in mind when they chose the names **Acadia Street** and **Uri Street.** The name "Acadia" is familiar to most Louisianians, especially those of Acadian descent. Acadia Parish is one of the sixty-four parishes of Louisiana. The Acadian people of Louisiana are the descendants of the French-speaking refugees who were expelled from the region of French Canada called "Acadie." "Acadia" is the

Latinized version of the name. The name is not, however, French, any more than "bayou" and "Tchoupitoulas" are French. Long before the French settled eastern Canada, the people who lived there, the Micmacs, called the land a name that the French settlers spelled "Acadie."

The origins of the name "Uri" are more complicated. Uri is a man's name in Hebrew, meaning "my light." The controversial Israeli-British illusionist and purveyor of the paranormal, Uri Geller, may be the best known Uri in the world.

"Uri" is also an ancient Germanic word meaning "bull." It is said to have derived from the word "aurochs," an extinct species of bison that once grazed in the meadows of the Alps. This word became the name of a region of Switzerland, Uri, which was one of the original members of the Swiss Confederation of 1291. It was the home of the legendary archer, William Tell. The canton, or state, of Uri continues today as part of Switzerland.

Drivers proceeding along **Acadia** and **Uri streets** can choose what they want the street names to mean. These names are a lot more interesting than something bland and uninspiring like **Causeway Boulevard** or **Clearview Parkway**.

As east Jefferson was growing and expanding in the 1960s, some developers had the idea of creating an entertainment district in Metairie, "New Metairie" as it was being called. They were hopeful that legalized gambling would be approved, and the new district of bars, night clubs, and restaurants would be the place for slot machines and even casinos. The anticipation was a couple of decades too early. It was not until "gambling" had a name change to "gaming" and the creation of the Louisiana Lottery that gambling, the legal version, would be seen in Jefferson Parish.

The idea of an entertainment district outside the French Quarter of New Orleans was enticing to developers and investors. Someone came up with the name "Fat City" for the project. In the early 1960s, the term "fat city" was slang for a condition, situation, or place in which someone was confident, satisfied, pleased. It is akin to the term "fat and sassy" or the jazzmen's "copacetic." If someone had achieved a goal, landed a desired job, or completed a project well, the person was said to be in "fat city." The term "city" in slang usage meant any state or condition in which a person might be. Bad luck was described as being in "dirt city" or a more scatological adjective. When an argument escalated from shouting to punching, the participants were said to have gone to "fist city." The word "city" was also used for commercial purposes, with automobile dealerships being named something like "Chevy City." The now-defunct nationwide electronics retail firm Circuit City was an outgrowth of the slang term. Fat City was supposed to light up the Metairie night with first-class entertainment.

A section of **Eighteenth Street** at the intersection with **Edenborn Avenue** became **Fat City Avenue,** but instead of becoming an appealing nighttime neighborhood, Fat City went to sleaze shortly after it was created, without ever passing through the stages of being high class. Eventually most of the joints that featured go-go girls and catered to guys with lots of gold chains closed up. Periodic efforts have been made to improve Fat City, but the image is there, probably for a very long time. Unfortunately, never could it be said that Metairie's Fat City was ever in fat city.

Edenborn Avenue gets its name from William Edenborn, a president of the Illinois Central Railroad, just as the city of Harahan was named for another of the railroad's presidents. One block west of **Edenborn Avenue** is **Hessmer Avenue;** Hessmer was named for William Edenborn's sister, Hessmer Edenborn.

Metairieites living on **Harang Avenue** need to explain that the name of their street is not a noisy speech; that is a "harangue," pronounced the same way. Rather, the street is named for Jean Murville Harang, the first president of the Jefferson Parish Police Jury in 1834. He was also the parish judge. The police jury had no police power and wasn't a jury; it was the governing body of the parish until the creation of the Jefferson Parish Council.

The main entrance to Lafreniere Park is via a street named **Downs Boulevard**. It connects to **Veterans Memorial Boulevard**. The name of the street is a remnant of the time that Lafreniere Park was a race track, Jefferson Downs. The track moved to Kenner, but it didn't last very long there either. Jefferson Downs was the last track in Jefferson Parish. Jefferson Park subdivision in Old Jefferson was once a race track. De Limon Place on **Metairie Road** was a dog-racing track at one time. **Downs Boulevard,** even long after the race track shut down, had a seedy reputation because of a notorious joint near the entrance to the park. Eventually, the parish council was able to shut down the Downs Lounge and demolish the building that was a hotbed of vice of all sorts, not a place parents bringing young children to soccer practice liked to see.

Here's a question for readers. Why are race tracks, once known as hippodromes, called "downs"? What's a "down," other than a term of football and soft feathers on a goose? Hint: it's not a let-down, a put-down, or a tie-down. There are two "down" streets in River Ridge, **Rosedown Place** and **Southdown Lane,** but both are named for old plantation houses, not race tracks.

Lafreniere Park, built on the site of the old race track, was named for an interesting and tragic figure in Louisiana history, Nicolas Chauvin de la Freniere. La Freniere was the son of one of the original founders, along with Jean-Baptiste le Moyne, Sieur de Bienville, of New Orleans and Louisiana. They were French Canadians of modest heritage. In the New World, their fathers could assume titles that would cause snickers had they tried to do the same in France. The title "La Freniere" most likely comes from the French word *frêne,* which means "ash tree." "La Freniere" thus means "a place with ash trees." Nicolas Chauvin de la Freniere was a landowner and leader in early Louisiana. He defied the Spanish authorities when they arrived in 1766 to take over the colony for Spain. He and his rebels packed Spanish Governor Antonio de Ulloa onto a ship and sent him away.

The king of Spain didn't like that rejection one bit and sent a new governor with lots of soldiers to put down the rebellion. Don Alejandro O'Reilly did not put up with la Freniere and his cohorts and had them shot, thus ending the threat to Spain's rule. The executed rebels were martyrs to the French people of New Orleans, and **Frenchmen Street** in the Faubourg Marigny is named for them. In Metairie not only is the park named for la Freniere, but so is **Lafreniere Street.**

A broad boulevard crosses Metairie from Lake Pontchartrain to **Airline Drive.** It was given the grandiose name of **Transcontinental Drive** even though it barely transects Metairie. Old plans show that the original route of the street was to continue south of **Airline Drive** and end at **Jefferson Highway** somewhere around where **Clearview Parkway** was later built. Before the road builders could get around to acquiring land and other necessary preparations to make **Transcontinental Drive** at least trans-east Jefferson, someone in the 1960s put a cemetery in the way between **Airline Drive** and the railroad tracks. Now drivers proceeding south on **Transcontinental Drive** must turn left or right upon reaching **Airline Drive** lest they wind up in the graveyard.

In that same neighborhood are two parallel streets, one block apart, whose names may make a traveler want to have a smoke. **Calumet Street** and **Camel Street** are just off the intersection of **Clearview Parkway** and **Airline Drive.** A "calumet" is a ceremonial pipe used by American Indians and, of course, "Camel" is the name of a popular brand of cigarettes. Light up. Smoke 'em if you got 'em. Cough, cough. The "coffin nails" can get someone into the graveyard, too.

West of Metairie lies the city of Kenner. Before going there, a Jefferson traveler should take a detour through the trees.

Trivia answer: By the way, a "down" is a grassy, slightly rolling open space. The word is British, and that may be where they raced horses.

Chapter 14
Tree Huggers

Naming streets for trees is usually a safe practice, uncontroversial, even pleasant. People generally like to live on streets whose names make them think of green and shade and a breeze passing through the leaves. It is no different in Jefferson Parish, where scores of streets are named for trees.

In Gretna between its city park and the Timberlane Country Club are streets named for trees, including **Cedar Lane, Maple Lane, Cypress Lane,** and **Elm Lane.** Also in Gretna are **Crape Myrtle Drive** and **Green Leaf Drive. Willow Lane, Willow Tree Drive,** and **Willow Drive** are all in Gretna, but they are not the same street. These multiple names sound like a recipe for confusion. If someone says, "I live on Willow in Gretna," a listener can't know which street is the correct one. None of the streets named Willow is designated as a "street," which may add to the confusion.

In Harvey, exotic trees are named on **Sandalwood Drive** and **Teakwood Drive.** Nearby are **Maple Avenue, Maplewood Drive, Beechwood Drive, Redwood Drive,** and **Dogwood Drive.**

Do not look for any citrus trees on **Citrus Boulevard** in the Elmwood industrial area of Old Jefferson. The landscapers lined the neutral ground with oak trees, which is probably a good idea. Motorists stopping to pick oranges and satsumas on a busy boulevard do not enhance traffic safety. **Citrus Boulevard** is an extension of **Citrus Road,** which begins near the Mississippi River levee in River Ridge, crosses the Soniat Canal into Harahan, and ends abruptly at **Hickory**

Avenue. Drivers must loop around on tiny **Vicknair Street** to **Dickory Avenue** in order to reach the beginning of **Citrus Boulevard**. **Citrus Lane** connects **Citrus Road** to **Orchard Road**, but there are no citrus trees on **Citrus Lane** either. And the orchards on **Orchard Road**? There aren't any.

Despite the absence of citrus trees on **Citrus Road**, **Citrus Lane**, and **Citrus Boulevard**, different types of citrus trees show up in the names of other Jefferson Parish streets. There are **Satsuma Street** and **Mandarin Street** in Metairie, **Orange Street** in River Ridge, and **Orange Lane** on Grand Isle. In Gretna, a motorist can drive on **Orange Blossom Drive**. **Lime Street** in Metairie is parallel to **Lemon Street**. In fact, there are two separate **Lemon Streets** in Metairie, one short street in Old Metairie and a long one between and parallel to **Transcontinental Drive** and **Clearview Parkway**.

The longer **Lemon Street** crosses **Veterans Memorial Boulevard**. At that corner there once was an automobile dealership that closed its gates forever. It is no wonder that the business is defunct. Who in the world would try to sell cars on a street called Lemon? No one has yet named a street in Jefferson Parish for a tangerine or a grapefruit; no Kumquat Street either. Do any readers know the origin of the name "satsuma" for the popular Louisiana citrus fruit?

Trees are not just pleasant to look at and to provide shade; some of their woods give off nice aromas. The odors must have been on the minds of the street namers of Harvey's **Cedar Street, Cypress Street, Camphor Drive,** and **Fir Court**. Nearby are nonaromatic **Beech Street** and **Cottonwood Street**. The leaves of bay trees provide nice aromas in bay rum and crab boil. The aromatic tree is remembered on **Sweet Bay Lane** in Waggaman.

Although it is not known for its aroma, **Chestnut Street** is also in the group with the aromatic trees, and the chestnut tree is closely related to the Chinkapin tree. South of Harvey and **Chestnut Street** is where **Chinkapin Street** can be found. The name is from the Algonquian American Indian language family.

Is it any surprise that the car dealership on Lemon Street is closed?

Elsewhere in Harvey, **Tallow Tree Lane** is named for an import from China, the Chinese tallow tree. There is a **Tallow Lane** on Grand Isle, too. One version of the history of the tree is that Benjamin Franklin brought specimens to the United States to use as an ornamental. The nuts of the tree were used in China for producing oil. The trees have flourished in Louisiana and have become a pest, crowding out native species. Naming a Jefferson Parish street **Tallow Tree Lane** is comparable to naming one Nutria Avenue.

Grand Isle is the only inhabited barrier island in Louisiana, and it is also the last remaining barrier island that has a forest. There is a nature preserve in the middle of the island that attracts migratory birds and migrating bird watchers. It is understandable that Grand Isle has lots of streets named for trees, but most of the names are of trees that do not grow there. Almost all the streets on Grand Isle are called lanes, with the exception of the only main street, **Louisiana Highway 1.** Connected to that highway are streets named **Cherry, Peach, Plum, Apricot, Fig, Mulberry, Apple,** and **Olive lanes,** all of which are fruit trees even if they don't grow on Grand Isle. Some other Grand Isle tree lanes are **Cedar, Palm, Elm, Cypress, Walnut, Pine, Birch,** and **Willow lanes.** Kenner likes these tree names, too, as evidenced by **Cypress Drive, Cedar Drive,** and **Elm Drive.**

There are some tree-named streets that should have been laid out parallel to or crossing another because of connections between their names. These streets are, however, not close to each other. Harahan's **Hickory Avenue** and Kenner's **Jackson Street** are miles apart. **Jackson Street** in Westwego is even farther, but at least it is on the same side of the river as Terrytown, where **Hickory Street** is one of several streets with names beginning with *H*. These streets should be closer to each other; General Andrew Jackson's nickname was Old Hickory. In River Ridge, **Joplin Street** is on the wrong side of the river with respect to **Maple Street** in Gretna and **Maple Street** in Westwego. The name of the composer of the "Maple Leaf Rag," Scott Joplin, should be nearby.

In Marrero, there are so many streets named for trees that the namers must have run out of names. Instead, there are streets named for parts of trees: **Twig Drive, Foliage Drive, Sprig Drive,** and **Bark Avenue.** Drivers can reach these streets by turning from the **Leo Kerner-Lafitte Parkway** onto a street named for a deformed tree, **Bent Tree Boulevard.**

Anyone living on **Yew Street** in Westwego should be prepared to answer the question: Do you have a ewe on **Yew Street**? It is appropriate to feel sheepish if the answer is yes.

Although there are **Magnolia Boulevard** in Harahan, **Appletree Lane** in Terrytown, and **Persimmon Avenue** in Metairie, by far the most popular tree that gets onto a name of a street is the oak. From **Oak Street** in Bucktown to **Oak Lane** in Grand Isle, the mighty oak gets crisscrossed across Jefferson Parish in many versions and manifestations. **Dueling Oaks Avenue** in Marrero, **Whispering Oaks Drive**

in River Ridge, and **Oak Grove Drive** in Metairie near
Lafreniere Park display some of the creativity in choosing
names for streets based on a universal appreciation of oak
trees.

Oak trees are holy. At least the pagan Celts and their
priests, the Druids, thought so. Although those ancient
Europeans worshipped a different type of oak from those
that grow in Jefferson Parish, when one looks upon a
magnificent, hundreds-years-old live oak, the grandeur
of the tree makes it easy to understand how someone
could consider it sacred. The pre-European inhabitants of
Jefferson Parish may not have considered oak trees divine,
but they made use of them. Acorns were shelled and ground
into a meal that was nutritious if not very tasty. The fallen
branches were used for firewood. The spreading limbs
gave shade. The tannin in the bark provided medicine. If
not sacred to contemporary Jeffersonians, oak trees are
certainly valuable. Oak trees are aesthetically pleasing and
photogenic. They shade homes from the sun, reduce the
need for air conditioning, and they bolster the monetary
value of a house.

There are several types of oak trees native to Jefferson
Parish. One of the most common is the water oak, and it
gets recognized on **Water Oaks Drive** in Waggaman. The
Nuttall's oak is often called a red oak; it has large acorns
and leaves with deep lobes and sharp points. Whether the
people who named **Red Oak Drive** in Oak Forest Estates in
Estelle or **Red Oak Drive** in Kenner knew about the Nuttall's
oak is not important. The name "**Red Oak Drive**" has better
rhythm and appeal than naming the street Nuttall's Oak
Drive.

The oak is so popular in Estelle that four separate
subdivisions connected to **Barataria Boulevard** are named
for it: Oak Cove, Barataria Oaks Estates, Oak Forest Estates,
and Oak Ridge.

The name "oak" goes well with other descriptive names
such that there are **Oak Ridge Boulevard** in Metairie

River Oaks Drive and **Oak Creek Road** in Old Jefferson, both near the intersection of **Dickory Avenue** and **Citrus Boulevard**; and **Southern Oak Drive** in Harvey. **Garden Oak Lane** and **Shady Oak Lane** are in River Ridge, and **Towering Oaks Avenue** is in Marrero. Marrero also has an **Oak Drive** nearly matched by Westwego's **Oak Street** and **Olde Oaks Drive**. In nearby Nine Mile Point there is **Oak Avenue**, and Harvey likes oaks, too, with **Glenoak Drive** and **Spanish Oaks Drive**. In Waggaman there is a pleasant residential street named **Laurel Oak Lane.**

Long ago there was a plantation called Oakland in what became Kenner. It is remembered in **Oakland Road** in Kenner and **Oakland Avenue** in Harahan. The Terrytown oaks are illustrated in **Green Oak Drive** and **Oakdale Drive.**

Oak trees are classified by dendrologists—they're the scientists who study trees—into two broad groups, red oaks and white oaks. However, depending on the location, oaks get local and regional names that become confusing. This confusion is the reason for scientific names of different species, using Latin. For example, the Nuttall's oak is also known as the red oak and the pin oak, but there are many others in the red oak group. The Southern red oak, *Quercus falcata,* is also called the Spanish oak or the swamp red oak. Farther north, the scarlet oak, *Quercus coccinea,* is called the red oak, too, but to add to the confusion, it is also called the black oak. Dendrologists aren't color blind, but local people give the same trees conflicting names.

The scientists who gave the Nuttall's oak its name weren't all a bunch of nuts; nor was the tree named for the nuts it produces. It is named for a biologist named Thomas Nuttall who lived from 1786 to 1859, but the tree did not get his name until 1927.

The specific white oak, *Quercus alba,* is not the only tree called a white oak. The Durand oak, *Quercus durandii,* is sometimes in some places called a white oak, too, and the Overcup oak, *Quercus lyrata,* gets called the water white oak as well. This discussion could go on through many more species and subspecies of oaks, but the impression to be made is that there are lots of oaks with lots of the same and different names.

Oak Avenue in Harahan is one block away and parallel to **Hickory Avenue**, which is a block from **Dickory Avenue**. A rhyme could be made to remember these adjacent streets:

Hickory, Dickory, Oak,
The mouse can't tell a joke.
The leaves blew away,
The mouse lost his way.
Hickory, Dickory, Oak.
No, that won't work, will it?

A drive through the Estelle subdivision entered through **Oak Forest Boulevard** can illustrate the many oaks available to give names to streets. Both general groups of oaks are represented on **Red Oak Drive** and **White Oak Drive**. There are also **Sweet Oak Drive** and **Liberty Oaks Drive**. The famous painter of birds, John James Audubon, has a street in his name, **Audubon Oaks Drive**. Parts of the oak tree provide the names for **Oak Leaf Drive** and **Acorn Street**. The name of **Pin Oak Drive** is one of those oak names that gets applied to many different species of oaks in different parts of the country.

The names **Oak Haven Drive** and **Chenier Street** state the obvious: The Oak Forest subdivision is a place of oaks. The word *chênier* comes from the basic French word for oak, *chêne,* and *chênier* means "a place of oaks." Jefferson Parish's southernmost community, Chênière Caminada, was once a place of many oaks, but the trees, the homes, the boats, and hundreds of people were lost in the great hurricane of 1893.

When most people in Jefferson Parish think of an oak tree, they envision the grandest species of all, the live oak. Everything about the tree speaks a language of power and strength, beauty and dignity, mystery and romance, protection and durability. Their distinctive wide canopies and dark, thick trunks make them instantly recognizable. Their low branches that reach out and meet the earth, like a flying buttress on a medieval cathedral, provide places for generations of children to climb. They are, in effect, natural cathedrals that exude a sensation of sanctity and the majesty of creation. It is no wonder the Druids worshipped the oaks.

The live oak, *Quercus virginiana,* is the densest, strongest tree in North America. One cubic foot of green wood from a live oak can weigh as much as seventy-seven pounds. Wood from the live oak was used in the construction of America's oldest, most famous warship, the USS *Constitution,* still in commission and afloat in Boston harbor. The live oak of the ship was its armor in the War of 1812, before iron and steel ships were made. British cannon balls bounced off the live-oak sides of the *Constitution* which gave it the nickname "Old Ironsides."

Live oaks live to be hundreds of years old. There are trees in New Orleans City Park that are remnants of a grove that grew on the end of the Bayou Metairie ridge. They are estimated to be six hundred years old. No one can give an accurate account of a live oak's age, however, unless there is a record of when it sprouted or was planted. The trees grow rapidly in their first fifty years, then slow down their growth. Some years there is no growth in the trunk, so the usual method of counting the growth rings is not reliable. Their low center of gravity, intricate and extensive root system, and great strength make them stand up well to even strong hurricanes. They may lose limbs and be partially broken, but the resilience of live oaks usually results in new branches shooting forth not long after any storm damage.

The live oaks of the cheniers in the coastal swamps and marshes are Jefferson Parish's initial defense against hurricanes. These strong trees absorb the storm's energy, dissipating the destructive power. Their root systems hold the earth and prevent the land from being scoured away. It is in tribute to these magnificent trees that so many streets have been named for them. **Live Oak Drive** is a fitting name for a street on Grand Isle, itself a large chenier with old live oaks in its center. **Live Oak Manor Drive** in Waggaman is the central street of a subdivision dedicated to the trees, Live Oak Manor. **Live Oak Boulevard** follows a route through a wooded area south of Waggaman.

Jefferson Parish is blessed with many fine old live oaks. Along **Metairie Road** and in other locations in Old Metairie are trees well over one hundred years old. On an old midden where **Barataria Boulevard** crosses Bayou Coquille in the Barataria Preserve near Crown Point, there is a grove of gnarled and battered live oaks, several hundred years old, whose green leaves and healthy shoots mock the abuse they have received from humans and nature. There are two magnificent specimens on short **Redgate Drive** in River Ridge.

Along and near the **River Road** in Old Jefferson on the east bank are many of the great trees, large specimens near the intersection of **Claiborne Court** and **Sundorn Street,** in the 200 block of **Dodge Avenue,** and especially at the site where the Elmwood Plantation manor house once stood. At the intersection of **Bridge City Avenue** and the **River Road** in Westwego there once stood a magnificent, stately plantation manor house called Seven Oaks. The manor house went into disrepair so severe that it had to be demolished, a tragic loss to history and culture. Some of the live oaks for which it was named are still there, sheltering the ghosts who weep at the loss.

When the Elmwood Plantation site was being developed for industrial use, the planners were so impressed with the lanes of live oaks growing there that they specifically protected them. They created **Brookhollow Esplanade,** a street connecting the **River Road** and **Jefferson Highway,** so that the trees are on land between the lanes of traffic. Another street, unnamed and private, one block upriver, has a row of the great trees somewhat protected. The name **Brookhollow Esplanade** seems almost inappropriate for a street filled with the beautiful oaks; there is no brook, there is no hollow. Why couldn't the street have been given a name for its beautiful reason for being, something like "Grand Oaks Avenue" or "Great Oaks Drive"?

The plantation was named Elmwood, but it is best known for its live oaks, there being no elms at Elmwood. Oaks are so popular and appealing that there is a retail center at the intersection of **Jefferson Highway** and **Clearview Parkway** called Elmwood Oaks. The street into the center is called **Elmwood Oaks Plaza.** On the Westbank, the Oakwood Center, wedged between Gretna and Terrytown, sticks with the oaks and doesn't say it is the "Oakwood Elms."

The names of **Oak Alley Boulevard** in Marrero and **Oak Alley** near the Metairie lakefront call to mind one of the most popular tourist attractions and film sites in Louisiana, Oak Alley Plantation in St. James Parish. Two long lines of old live oaks create the spectacular alley for which the plantation is named.

Live oaks are so revered that they have an exclusive club. Only hundred-year-old and older live oaks can become members of the Live Oak Society. The trees are nominated, by name, by a human sponsor, and they are then entered into the registry of the Live Oak Society. Even those trees that die or—heaven forbid—are destroyed remain on the registry.

When a great live oak is threatened, the oak huggers spring into action. One of Jefferson Parish's oldest oaks is located on the edge of the planned route of the extension of **Dickory Avenue** in Old Jefferson at the edge of Harahan. The grading and digging required to build the road, a state highway, would have come perilously close to the old oak, damaging its root system. Tree lovers united in opposition; the governor personally stepped in and ordered the highway department to move the roadbed a sufficient distance so that the tree would not be harmed. A plaque was erected near the tree proclaiming that it was already growing when Christopher Columbus arrived in the Western Hemisphere although there is no historical or scientific evidence to confirm that assertion. Nevertheless, the tree is very old, very large, and is emblematic of the affection Jeffersonians have for live oaks. To see the great oak, proceed south on **Dickory Avenue** from **Citrus Boulevard,** turn left on **Hickory Ridge Lane,** then right on **Ferriday Court.** The oak is surrounded by a low, white fence that gives the sense of a sanctuary. It is; the live oak is holy.

Shortly after the successful defense of the old oak, the Jefferson Parish streets department erected special signs at the entrance to Old Jefferson on **Clearview Parkway, Citrus Boulevard, Jefferson Highway** at the Harahan city limits, and the **River Road.** The signs inform drivers that they are entering Old Jefferson, with a silhouette of an old live oak to illustrate what is important in Jefferson.

Trivia answer: Satsuma is a region of the Japanese island Kyushu, the southernmost of the main islands of Japan.

Chapter 15
Kenner

Who in the world would name their child Minor? Mr. and Mrs. William Kenner Sr. did. In the twenty-first century, giving a child a name at his birth suggesting that he is second rate, grade *B,* and a loser would strike some people as being child abuse. After all, with a name like that he is liable to grow up with low self-esteem, feeling inadequate, a male Cinderella so to speak. But that didn't happen to Minor Kenner.

Minor Kenner was born more than two hundred years ago, and his name comes from his mother's family name, Minor. Despite being Minor, he was not a minor child, the first son in a family of eleven children. William Kenner Sr. was a successful planter and commercial entrepreneur in New Orleans and along the Mississippi River. He was a leader of a militia who fought at the Battle of New Orleans. His four sons were Minor, William Butler, George R., and Duncan F. Kenner, and they acquired land upriver from the Tchoupitoulas Coast known as *Cannes Brûlée,* "Burnt Canes" in English. The Brothers Kenner would establish themselves as planters and entrepreneurs, too. They took over the Oakland Plantation upriver from where **Williams Boulevard** ends at the levee. Two other adjacent plantations, Belle Grove and Pasture Plantations, eventually were owned by one or more of the Kenners.

With the coming of the railroad and the wealth from sugar, Minor Kenner saw an opportunity to create a town accessible to New Orleans but far enough away to escape the filth and the pestilence—yellow fever—that plagued the booming city. In 1855, Minor Kenner became the major player in the creation of the city of Kenner when he hired a surveyor to lay out a grid of streets on some of the plantation lands. Those streets and many of their names continue today.

The 1855 map shows a street named for the developer, **Minor Street.** He also named one for his father and his brother, who had died of yellow fever in 1853, **William Street.** Downriver from those streets, Minor's choice of names reveals a lot about his political feelings. His choices signal that, although he and his brothers were wealthy landowners and employed many slaves, his political heroes were men who favored a strong, undivided federal government, even as the South was heading for secession.

Jackson Street honors Andrew Jackson, hero of the Battle of New Orleans and the seventh president of the United States, serving from 1829 to 1837. Jackson was a southerner and slave owner, too, but he was vehemently against secession and the weakening of the country for which he had won a great victory. On April 13, 1830, Jackson made his point with a toast at the Jefferson Day dinner in Washington: "Our Federal union! It must be preserved!"

President Zachary Taylor, like Jackson, was a former general, a hero of the war with Mexico, a southerner and slave owner, and a fierce supporter of the union. He is remembered on Kenner's **Taylor Street.** Taylor died after less than two years in office, 1849-1850, and was succeeded by his vice president, the hapless Millard Fillmore. Minor Kenner must have felt some appreciation for the last Whig president because he named a street at the edge of Kenner for him, **Filmore Street.** It is unclear whether Minor Kenner or subsequent officials wrote Millard Fillmore's (with two *L*s) name on the street **Filmore** (with one *L*).

Another political figure of that era was Senator Henry Clay of Kentucky, also a dedicated unionist. He is studied in American history as the "Great Compromiser," the man who negotiated legislation that would keep the southern slave owners and the northern abolitionists at least in agreement if not pleased. He is best known for the series of legislation known as the Compromise of 1850. His effort stalled secession for ten more years before the tragedy of the Civil War. Minor Kenner honored Henry Clay by naming two of the streets on his grid **Clay Street** and **Compromise Street.** The Kenner brothers were so impressed by Henry Clay that Duncan Kenner, the youngest brother who became rich in the sugar business, named his plantation in Ascension Parish Ashland, after Clay's home in Kentucky. There is no street in Kenner named for Ashland, but Terrytown has an **Ashland Place.**

Another champion of federal supremacy, Daniel Webster, senator from Massachusetts, is also named in the original plan of Kenner, **Webster Street.** Although opposed to slavery, Webster joined with the compromisers of 1850 to preserve the union, heeding President Jackson's toast of twenty years earlier. After President Taylor died, Webster became secretary of state under President Fillmore in 1850 and then died in 1852.

On the north side of the railroad tracks, running north and south, is a street named for another famous statesman of the pre-Civil War era. John C. Calhoun, senator from South Carolina, was on the opposite side of issues from Daniel Webster and others who favored a strong federal government. Calhoun was a champion of states' rights and promoter of the doctrine of nullification by which the states could nullify acts of Congress. He died before the secessions that led to the Civil War, but he saw secession only as an act of last resort to protect individual states' sovereignty. John C. Calhoun is remembered on **Calhoun Street** in Kenner.

Minor Kenner must not have had much trust in the man who was president at the time he planned his city in 1855 because there is no street in Kenner named for Franklin Pierce.

Upriver from **Minor Street** is **Daniel Street,** and it is not clear whether Minor Kenner named it for Daniel Webster, too. **Oxley Street** is named for Minor's brother-in-law, Charles Oxley, husband of Minor's sister Martha Kenner Oxley.

How many modern real-estate developers would name a street for their mother-in-law? If the mother-in-law were the source of the land, it might be a good idea. Minor Kenner acquired the Belle Grove Plantation through his wife, Eliza, who inherited it from her mother, Maria Holliday. From that line of inheritance comes **Maria Street**. Parallel to that street are **Duncan Street, Butler Street,** and **George Street,** named for the other brothers, Duncan Kenner, William Butler Kenner, and George R. Kenner. Thus, as drivers proceed along **Jefferson Highway,** they can study Kenner history at each cross street.

Wait a minute! **Jefferson Highway.** doesn't go through that part of Kenner. Or does it? As you leave River Ridge heading west and enter Kenner on **Jefferson Highway,** the road, **Louisiana Highway 48,** becomes **Reverend Richard Wilson Drive.** The state legislature changed the name of the roadway in 2003 to honor the memory of the pastor of the Pilgrim Baptist Church. Pastor Wilson led his flock to become one of the most active churches in Kenner, moving and expanding it to the current site in the Rivertown historic district on the street that now bears his name.

But before it became **Reverend Richard Wilson Drive,** the street was not **Jefferson Highway,** even though it is the same state highway and a continuation from River Ridge. Before 2003, long before, the street was **Third Street.** The reason for the different name is that **Third Street** was laid out and named before **Jefferson Highway** came into existence. In 1855 Minor Kenner gave number names to the east-west streets running perpendicular to the streets named for his family and political heroes. Today **Reverend Richard Wilson Drive** (formerly **Third Street**) is the final street before the Mississippi River levee. Minor Kenner's grid had **First Street** and **Second Street,** but they no longer exist. The movement of the batture by the river and

Don't believe it! The cross street at the end of Williams Boulevard is Reverend Richard Wilson Drive.

especially the construction of the current setback levee in the 1930s destroyed those two streets.

As it proceeds west, upriver, **Reverend Richard Wilson Drive** undergoes another name change. Or perhaps it is more correct to say that the street reverts to its older name, **Third Street**. This occurs at the intersection of **Pollock Place**. **Louisiana Highway 48** remains **Third Street** until it reaches the St. Charles Parish line, at which it becomes the **River Road**.

If all those name changes aren't enough to bewilder drivers unfamiliar with south Kenner, there is a street sign attached to the traffic signal light at the end of **Williams Boulevard** at Rivertown that adds to the confusion. The sign identifies the cross street as **Jefferson Highway**. But it isn't. The street at that point is **Reverend Richard Wilson Drive**. A driver can get to **Jefferson Highway** by turning left and driving several blocks to the Kenner city limit at River

Ridge. **Jefferson Highway** is the name of the roadway at that point and eastward.

Minor Kenner's 1855 map shows **William Street** in the same location as modern **Williams Boulevard.** How did the additional *S* get affixed to William's name? Perhaps it was just that people were using the possessive form of the name in speaking and saying "William's Street." Or maybe the *S* sound at the beginning of "street" fused with "William" to the point that people were saying "Williams Street" for "William Street." Whatever the reason, **Williams Boulevard,** the current designation of **William Street,** is the major north-south street in the city of Kenner, a fact that would probably please someone named Minor.

The Louis Armstrong International Airport is owned by the city of New Orleans, but it is physically located in the city of Kenner. New Orleans honors its most famous native son, musician, and entertainer by naming the airport after him. The city of Kenner has honored its less-well-known native son, musician, and entertainer, Lloyd Price, by naming a portion of **Fourth Street** in the Rivertown historic district **Lloyd Price Avenue.** Price is best known for his rhythm and blues song "Personality."

The airport was originally named Moisant Airport, and it is still sometimes referred to as Moisant Field. It was named for John B. Moisant, an aviation pioneer who crashed and died on the site of the future airport on December 31, 1910. Moisant was a participant in an endurance race, but his airplane was not up to the task. The site of his death became a stockyard, and in a somewhat macabre tribute, it was named the Moisant Stockyard. It was macabre because part of a stockyard's operation is an abattoir, a slaughterhouse. Not only did John B. Moisant die there, so did a lot of animals. The initials for Moisant Stockyard, MSY, became the international symbol for the airport. That symbol continues today. Travelers should try not to remember that the airport's symbol stands for an airplane crash and a lot of slaughtered animals. Kenner remembers

John B. Moisant and his tragic death by naming **Moisant Street** for the aviator.

A drive along **Joe Yenni Boulevard, West Esplanade Avenue,** and **Thirty-Second Street** eastward from the Duncan Canal provides the opportunity to observe the names of the cross streets and get a clue to when those streets were named. Beginning with **Alabama Avenue,** the streets are named for the states in alphabetical order, excluding Louisiana. The alphabetical sequence ends when **Minnesota Avenue** is reached. Nevertheless, someone wanted to make sure that Tennessee and Texas were included, so there are **Tennessee Avenue** and **Texas Avenue** as well. A couple of states' names that should be part of the alphabetical order are missing, Hawaii and Alaska. Their absence from the grid shows that the streets were given their names before 1959, the year those two states were admitted to the union. Nevertheless, there is an **Alaska Street** in Westwego. It runs parallel to, one block apart, **Texas Street,** honoring the two geographically largest states in the union. Westwego thinks big.

In 2009, PBS showed a ten-hour documentary series called *The National Parks: America's Best Idea.* Many Americans agree with that title, and in the northwest corner of Kenner, there is a subdivision whose streets are named for some of the national parks. The developers thought that national parks were a good idea, too, because some of the streets are named for the best-known parks in the West, including **Yellowstone Street, Yosemite Street,** and **Glacier Street.** Popular parks in the eastern United States are there, too: **Shenandoah Street** and **Everglades Street. Guadalupe Street** is named for Guadalupe Mountains National Park in Texas, and **Carlsbad Street** for Carlsbad Caverns National Park in New Mexico. The magnificent canyon of the Zion National Park in Utah is the namesake for **Zion Street.** Colorado's Mesa Verde National Park was established to protect and preserve the ancient dwellings built into the cliff sides hundreds of years before the Europeans arrived in North America. **Mesa Verde Street** gets its name from that park.

There are almost four hundred separate sites in the National Park system today, and there were fewer but still many to choose from when the streets were named. The parks chosen show that the developers were careful about which parks would appeal to potential home buyers. Choosing streets with names like "Alcatraz," "Death Valley," "Badlands," "Devil's Postpile," and "Trail of Tears," all parts of the National Park system, would be a case study in bad marketing. **Sequoia Street** and **Olympic Street**, named for parks in California and Washington, respectively, give a much better image.

In north Kenner, in the vicinity of the Chateau Country Club, many of the streets were named by oenophiles. That's a fancy word for wine lovers. Or maybe the real-estate promoters had read St. Paul's first letter to Timothy in which St. Paul advises his friend to drink wine for his stomach's sake. One can imagine real-estate planners poring over grids and charts, all the while sampling wines from several regions of France, swirling the wine in glasses and observing the body, bouquet, ullage, and all those other things that wine people do to avoid saying how the wine tastes.

Some of the wine streets have names familiar to people who simply enjoy a bottle of wine: **Rhone Drive** and **Loire Drive** recall rivers in France whose valleys support lots of vineyards. Vouvray is one of the famous wines of the Loire Valley, and it gets a street in Kenner, too, **Vouvray Drive.** **Bordeaux Drive** gets its name from a major wine-producing region of France. And then there are the more exotic, less familiar names of wines and vineyards. **Fleurie Drive** is named for a Beaujolais wine; **Carmenere Drive** is from a red wine made in Chile. The Alsatian wine-growing region of France is recognized on **Clevner Drive** and **Traminer Drive.** Sylvaner is another grape of the Alsace region; it is also popular in Germany and Austria. **Sylvaner Drive** celebrates this white wine.

The Burgundy region is recognized in the name of **Echezeaux Drive,** a section of Burgundy known for fine estate wines, and the wine-making city of Beaune, France, on **Beaune Drive.** Other Kenner streets where one can sip wines and describe their taste in outrageous verbiage ("notes of pomegranate and Moroccan leather . . .") are **Brouilly Drive, Montrachet Drive, Chablis Drive, Tavel Drive,** and **Pommard Drive.**

Probably there was no spell-check for wine names when the streets were named, most likely to the sound of a cork popping, because, like a few other streets in Jefferson Parish, **Petit Berdot Drive** is one letter off from what was intended. There is a wine in France called Petit Verdot, but no Petit Berdot. About the time the street was named, French film actress and sex symbol Brigitte Bardot was still a hot item in the world of entertainment. Who knows whether the street namers were thinking of her while they quaffed glasses of Petit Verdot. There was a French painter of the seventeenth century, Jean-Georges Berdot, but the namers may never have heard of him. Concern about the proper spelling of Kenner street names can be smoothed over by motoring over to **Champagne Drive** and opening a bottle of the bubbly. *À votre santé, mes amis.*

Streets adjacent to Chateau Country Club have names for, what else, some of the elegant chateaux (or chateaus) of France whose names are synonymous with fine wine. **Chateau Rothchild Drive** is named for one of the best-known estates in the Bordeaux region of France. If **Chateau Mouton Drive** were written in English it would be "Sheep Castle Drive." Such names are best left in the original language, especially when drinking the wine.

Other names for chateau streets come from estates of the Bordeaux region. **Chateau Magdelaine Drive, Chateau Haut Brion Drive,** and **Chateau Margaux Drive** are all very fine wines. From the Saint-Emilion section of Bordeaux comes **Chateau Ausone Drive.** The Médoc region of Bordeaux is where **Chateau Pontet Canet Drive** gets its name, and there is also a **Medoc Drive** in that neighborhood.

Obviously, those who picked the names of the wine

streets of Kenner were people who knew their wines. They were interested in attracting homebuyers who had enough disposable income that perhaps they, too, had become interested in fine, imported wines. There is a cachet of class and social power associated with knowledge of fine wine. It would have been interesting if the home sellers had attracted potential buyers with real-estate advertising inspired by labels on wine bottles. Here's a hypothetical example:

FOR SALE. Exquisite cottage in the vineyards of North Kenner. A first glance at this robust, rich home brings a blush of raspberries and orange-rind shutters, with a smooth coloring of Medoc-red bricks, and broad dormer windows lighting interior spaces to produce a bold finish with hints of Old Westwego. Notes of mirliton vine and green okra permeate the open space.

The choice of wine names for streets was obviously carefully planned. Even though the streets are named for wine, the planners wouldn't dare name them for street wines, the beverages of choice of those who spend their days (and nights) in the streets and those who bring refreshment to Mardi Gras parades. There are thus, in the wine country of north Kenner, no Thunderbird Street, Roma Rocket Road, Nighttrain Lane, White Port Place, or Boone's Farm Boulevard. No one would buy a house whose address is a street named M/D 20/20 Avenue. Nevertheless, in River Ridge, several miles from Kenner's fantasy vineyards, there is a **Ripple Road.** Pack a bottle of Annie Green Springs and head out to the parade.

Gretna has **Gretna Boulevard,** Old Jefferson has **Jefferson Street,** Old Metairie has **Metairie Road,** and the town of Jean Lafitte has **Jean Lafitte Boulevard.** Do any readers know if there is an equivalent street in Kenner?

Trivia answer: Kenner has **Kenner Avenue,** a modest street that runs along the north side of the railroad tracks.

Chapter 16
Higher Education

There is no main campus of any institution of higher learning in Jefferson Parish. There are branches of Tulane University, Delgado Community College, the University of New Orleans, and some online schools, but no place that has the feel of a four-year college campus. Jeffersonians are generally a well-educated group, and it may be that the absence of a college or university in the parish has inspired the names of streets in those who had good memories of their college years. The names also are used to attract better-educated prospective buyers. There are many streets in Jefferson Parish whose names are those of colleges and universities from all over the United States and some international ones, too.

Turning off **Barataria Boulevard** onto **College Parkway** in Estelle brings you into a subdivision whose streets are named, for the most part, for private, liberal-arts schools. **Bennington Drive** is near the entrance to the subdivision, named for renowned—and expensive—Bennington College in Bennington, Vermont. Also in Vermont and also expensive is Middlebury College in Middlebury. **Middlebury Street** is also near the entrance on **College Parkway.**

Grinnell Drive is named for Grinnell College in Grinnell, Iowa; and **Reed Street** is named for Reed College in Portland, Oregon. The pride of Ithaca, New York, is represented on **Cornell Drive.** Cornell University has one of the finest schools of hotel management, and its ornithology department is esteemed by bird watchers throughout the world. Other colleges and universities in the state of New York are named on **Syracuse Street, Vassar Street, Skidmore Street,** and **Rochester Drive.** The state of Pennsylvania's Swarthmore College is represented on **Swarthmore Street.**

There is a French connection in that subdivision as well. Most fine American colleges and universities have arrangements with schools in Europe for the American students to study for a summer, a semester, or a year at the European institution. **Lille Drive** gets its name from a city in France with several colleges. The University of Grenoble is well respected beyond France, throughout the world, including on **Grenoble Court** in Estelle. Colleges in Rennes, France, have connection with several American schools, as **Rennes Drive** attests.

The most prestigious university in France, at least to many Americans, is the University of Paris-Sorbonne, or Paris-Sorbonne University. It did not miss being called upon to provide a street's name, **Sorbonne Drive.** The city of Lyon, France, is often spelled "Lyons" in English, with no connection to the Lions Clubs International. It is a university town, and that may be the basis of the name of **Lyons Court,** but there is also a small liberal-arts college in Batesville, Arkansas, called Lyon College.

In Carroll County, Georgia, there once was a small school called Bowdon College. It closed in 1936, long before the Estelle subdivision was laid out. Nonetheless, there is a **Bowdon Street** among all the streets named for liberal-arts colleges that are still open. In Maine there is an excellent liberal-arts institution called Bowdoin College. Could it be that the street namers intended **Bowdon Street** to be named for the existing, prestigious college in Maine rather than the defunct school in Georgia? A missing *i* from the name could have changed the intent of the planners.

All these private and hard-to-get-into colleges charge a lot of tuition and fees for the privilege of attending. Combining just one academic year's cost of tuition at all the schools named in the subdivision connected to **College Parkway** could provide enough money for a retirement pension.

Maybe the people who named the streets were hoping to make enough from their enterprise and investment to send their children to one of those fine schools—at least for one year.

There used to be practices in the real-estate-sales business, now illegal, called steering and redlining. These were racially motivated actions to keep people of color from purchasing houses in certain neighborhoods. They were practiced after "whites only" covenants in land titles were declared illegal. As the African-American middle class grew and searched for pleasant, affordable housing, some developers decided to capitalize on the educational achievements of the black middle class and established subdivisions designed to attract this growing part of the real-estate market. One of those developments is Kennedy Heights in Waggaman on the Westbank.

A gimmick used to attract middle-class African-Americans to the real-estate market was to name some of the streets of Kennedy Heights for some of the historically black colleges and universities. In that subdivision are streets named for the three traditionally black universities in New Orleans, **Xavier Drive, Dillard Drive,** and **Southern Court.** The name Southern can apply equally to Southern University in Baton Rouge or Southern University in New Orleans. **Grambling Street** is named for Grambling State University in the north Louisiana city of Grambling. There is a **Prairieview Court,** recognizing Prairie View A & M University, the traditionally black school in Prairie View, Texas, **Morgan Court** gets its name from Morgan State University in Baltimore. One can study a small piece of the history of race relations simply by reading the street name signs.

In 1960 a generous benefactor gave Loyola University a large tract of land in Kenner between the airport and Lake Pontchartrain. At the time it was mostly marsh, and **Interstate 10** was just an idea. Immediately the rumor began that Loyola University was going to move its campus from

St. Charles Avenue in New Orleans to the Kenner location. The rumor increased the property values as developers envisioned selling homes to a well-educated clientele with above-average incomes, those who would be attracted by the idea of living in a university neighborhood. Whether the move was ever seriously contemplated by the Jesuits who own Loyola University, it did not take place. The tract was nonetheless called University City, and streets and infrastructure were established.

The main street into and through the development was named, appropriately enough, **Loyola Drive**, with two northern branches, **East Loyola Drive** and **West Loyola Drive**. In between the streets is an area that was made into a hospital, not a university. Loyola University's uptown neighbor is named as part of University City, **Tulane Drive**. Louisiana's largest university gets its full name on a street, **Louisiana State Drive**, not merely "LSU Drive." The University of Mississippi, however, gets a street in its more familiar name, **Ole Miss Drive**.

From south to north, beginning at **Veterans Memorial Boulevard**, streets in University City are named in alphabetical order for many different colleges and universities, public, private, and church-affiliated. Beginning with **Auburn Drive** and continuing through **Baylor Drive**, **Clemson Drive**, and **Duke Drive**, the street names proceed to **East Rice Place** and **West Rice Place**. Once called Alabama Polytechnic Institute, Auburn University is a public university located in Auburn, Alabama. Baylor University in Waco, Texas, is a school affiliated with the Southern Baptist Convention. Clemson is a state school in Clemson, South Carolina. Duke University is a private institution in Durham, North Carolina, and Rice University is a private school in Houston, Texas.

Other streets in the University City subdivision are **Emerson Drive** and **Furman Drive**. Emerson University is a private institution in Boston that emphasizes the arts and communication. Furman University is also private, a small school in Greenville, South Carolina. **Georgetown Drive** salutes the Jesuit school located in the neighborhood of the same name in Washington, D.C. There is another **Georgetown Drive** in Waggaman, named for the neighborhood, not the university.

The College of the Holy Cross is another school run by the Jesuit order; its campus is in Worcester, Massachusetts, and is remembered in University City on **Holy Cross Drive.** The planners added an additional "H" to the list of streets, **Houston Place,** named for the University of Houston in Texas. Another Catholic university, the University of the Incarnate Word, which is in San Antonio, Texas, gets its name on the street signs on **Incarnate Word Drive.**

Johns Hopkins University is a prestigious private university in Baltimore and is the inspiration for **Johns Hopkins Drive.** The Kilgore Rangerettes drill team is what Kilgore College is best known for. This community college in Kilgore, Texas, provides the name for **Kilgore Place.**

Miami Place may be named for two institutions, Miami University in Oxford, Ohio, and the University of Miami in Coral Gables, Florida. The former is a public school; the latter is private. From the colleges beginning with *M*, the University City planners chose two more, Millsaps College and Marquette University, to name **Millsaps Place** and **Marquette Drive.** Millsaps is a small, private college in Jackson, Mississippi; Marquette is a Jesuit school in Milwaukee, Wisconsin. There is a street with the same name in Harahan, **Marquette Street.**

The golden dome of the University of Notre Dame is not readily apparent on **East Notre Dame Place** and **West Notre Dame Place,** streets named for the best-known Catholic university in the country. There is also a **Rue Notre Dame** in Terrytown, but that street is named for the cathedral in the heart of Paris, not for the school near South Bend, Indiana, with the same name in French, but which calls its sports teams the "Fighting Irish."

The College of William & Mary, a public institution at

Williamsburg, Virginia, is named on **William and Mary Place**. Yet another Catholic center of learning, Villanova, has its name on **Villanova Place** in Kenner, far from its home in suburban Philadelphia. James Oglethorpe, the founding father of the state of Georgia, has a small, private school in Atlanta, named for him, Oglethorpe University, which in turn provides the name for **Oglethorpe Place**.

Davidson College, the prestigious liberal-arts college affiliated with the Presbyterian Church, situated near Charlotte, North Carolina, gives its name to **Davidson Place**. The acclaimed Ivy League institution Yale University in New Haven, Connecticut, is named on **Yale Drive** in University City and **Yale Avenue** in Metairie. Another Ivy League school, Princeton University of Princeton, New Jersey, is the source for the name of **Princeton Place**. Bradley University, a private school in Peoria, Illinois, is part of University City on **Bradley Place**.

The next street is **Colgate Place**, named not for toothpaste but for Colgate University in Hamilton, New York, a private, liberal-arts school. Temple University, a public institution in Philadelphia is named on **East** and **West Temple Place**. The highly respected private university in Palo Alto, California, is the inspiration for **East** and **West Stanford Place**.

Once a female-only Ivy League school, Vassar College in Poughkeepsie, New York, is now coeducational and gives the name to **Vassar Court**. Nearby is **Wake Forest Court**, from Wake Forest University, in Winston-Salem, North Carolina. Wake Forest is affiliated with the Baptist Church, but its mascots' name evokes the Satanic hosts in the oxymoronic Demon Deacons.

Northwestern Drive is located in the northwestern part of Jefferson Parish in University City, but its name comes from Northwestern University, the private university in Evanston, Illinois. The nation's most honored institution of higher learning, Harvard University, is not named in University City. There are, however, **Harvard Avenue**

in Metairie and **Harvard Avenue** and **Harvard Lane** in Terrytown. Also in Terrytown is the name of another Ivy League school, Dartmouth College of Hanover, New Hampshire, on **Dartmouth Street.** Terrytown did not miss the Jesuits and their dedication to higher education because **Fordham Place** has the name of Fordham University in New York City. Purdue University in West Lafayette, Indiana, was founded as a technical, science, and engineering school. It counts several astronauts among its alumni. It is recognized in Metairie on **Purdue Drive.**

One of the oldest, most respected universities in the world is named for a place where cattle once crossed a river. Its name shows up on two streets in Jefferson Parish, **Oxford Street** in Kenner and **Oxford Place** in Terrytown.

As has been mentioned previously, the choice of the name of a street in a residential housing development is largely a function of marketing. Unpleasant or strange-sounding names will not attract homebuyers, at least not the ones the developers are seeking. For this reason, perhaps, there is no Slippery Rock Road in Jefferson Parish, and Slippery Rock University in western Pennsylvania will continue to bring forth giggles, not home buyers. A similar remark is appropriate for Harvey Mudd College in Claremont, California, a private, liberal-arts school that will forever bear the brunt of the tired cliché, "It's name is Mudd." There is a **Harvey Boulevard** in Harvey, but no Harvey Mudd Street.

Chapter 17

Grand Isle

Grand Isle is the end of the road. Literally. **Louisiana Highway 1** goes south along the western side of Bayou Lafourche, crosses the bayou at Leeville, and proceeds south again to Port Fourchon before turning east into Jefferson Parish to Chênière Caminada. At Chênière Caminada the highway crosses Caminada Pass on a two-lane bridge and reaches Grand Isle on the other side. There are eight more miles before the road ends somewhat ignominiously at some old storage tanks on the edge of Bayou Rigaud.

Anyone who has heard of Grand Isle knows that it is rich in history, legend, mystery, and tragedy. It was not included in 1825 when the legislature created Jefferson Parish. The joining of Grand Isle to Jefferson took place in 1827 when Grand Isle was annexed out of Lafourche Parish. Although now part of Jefferson Parish, it is far removed geographically and culturally from the suburbia of Metairie and Terrytown. To get to Grand Isle a traveler must leave Jefferson Parish and drive through St. Charles and Lafourche parishes before arriving at the island two hours later.

Geologically, Grand Isle is very, very young. It is a barrier island that is no older than the Mayan ruins of Central America and the Yucatan Peninsula. When the Normans were invading England in 1066, the formation of Grand Isle was likely just beginning. Like all land forming the southeastern Louisiana coast, it was created by the Mississippi River. Bayou Lafourche was once the main channel of the river, and it created a broad delta from the silt dropped onto the continental shelf. That delta began to deteriorate when the river shifted course to its current channel. Currents along the shore moved the silt sand to form barrier islands, of which Grand Isle is one of the largest. The creation of Grand Isle is just a quick blink in geological time. In contrast, just across Lake Pontchartrain from Jefferson Parish, the north shore of the lake is a formation called by geologists the Pleistocene Terrace. It is several million years old. Today Grand Isle is the only permanently inhabited barrier island in Louisiana. It is also the last barrier island with a significant forested area, one that attracts birds migrating from winter homes in Central and South America.

Checking the street names on Grand Isle provides clues to its colorful history. Near the center of the island is **Coulon Rigaud Lane,** named for two of the earliest French families to settle there. The earliest record of a real-estate transaction on Grand Isle was a grant from the Spanish colonial governor, Bernardo de Gálvez, to an immigrant from Bordeaux, France, Jacques François Rigaud, dated July 2, 1781. Oral tradition holds that the first Rigaud—he may have been the same man—came to Grand Isle on September 2, 1758, before the transfer of Louisiana from France to Spain. Monsieur Rigaud married another French immigrant, Marie Durand, and their daughter, Thérèse Rigaud, married Pierre Coulon, a man who came to Grand Isle from Marseilles, France. Thus began a line of Rigauds and Coulons on Grand Isle that continues today through more than two hundred years and many generations.

Do not expect to see Grand Isle residents eating humble pie or displaying other signs of humility, even though there is a street on the island with the humble name of **Humble Road.** The origin of that name goes back to the mid-nineteenth century in east Texas near what was then the small town of Houston. A gentleman with the pleasant name of Pleasant Smith Humble (What were his parents thinking?) established a branch of the post office in his house. Soon the hamlet around his home became known as Humble because of the mail sent there. Then one day oil began to gush out of the ground; the Texas oil boom had begun. The town gave its name to the Humble Oil Company, which grew and thrived and had a sizable operation on Grand Isle for many years. Hence, **Humble Road** was named for the oil company that had been named for the town that had been named for Pleasant Smith Humble. Years later, Humble Oil Company was absorbed into Exxon-Mobil.

Nineteenth-century Grand Isle was a time of grand resort hotels, where the gentry from New Orleans and other hot, muggy, smelly cites would come for fresh sea breezes and relaxation. The romance of those times was depicted by novelist Kate Chopin in her eyebrow-raising story of a married woman falling in love with another man on Grand Isle. The novel, *The Awakening,* remains widely read today, partly because it describes the elegant life of the island, an era destroyed by the hurricane of 1893.

Nineteenth-century writer Lafcadio Hearn's novella about Grand Isle and the nearby coast, *Chita,* tells the tragic story of the hurricane of 1856 that destroyed *Isle Dernière,* Last Island, and the people who were lost and orphaned. Like Last Island in 1856, Grand Isle was forever changed by the 1893 hurricane. Hundreds of citizens of Chênière Caminada were killed, the hotels and bath houses of Grand Isle were destroyed, homes and businesses were lost, and there was an air of despair on the island in that time before FEMA.

In the center of Grand Isle, **Ludwig Lane** commemorates the man who led the islanders out of their post-hurricane desperation and changed the economy of the community. Predicting that the golden age of luxury hotels was over on Grand Isle, John Ludwig taught his neighbors commercial agriculture, creating many small farms that thrived in the subtropical atmosphere that once attracted resort tourists. Ludwig became known as King John because of his inspirational leadership and innovative ideas. He had the islanders use crushed shrimp shells, a readily available resource, to fertilize the sandy soil. He built what would become the largest terrapin farm in the country, selling the turtles to markets and restaurants far away.

Dr. Theodore Engelbach, a sickly physician told he was only a few months from death, moved to Grand Isle in 1901 to die peacefully. He didn't. Instead, he recovered and fell in love with the magical island and served as its doctor for forty more years. Engelbach also served as the justice of the peace. Today his name continues on **Engelbach Lane**. **Minnich Lane** recalls John Minnich, a prominent islander, carpenter and fisherman of the nineteenth century.

Formal, official names for the streets of Grand Isle did not come until the second half of the twentieth century. There was no main highway when the first bridge to the mainland across Caminada Pass was built in the early 1930s. Vehicles drove along the beach, the sand being compressed by the high tides and surf. In that time before air conditioning, there was little habitation between the trees in the center of the island and the edge of the Gulf of Mexico. The pathways and lanes from the structures under the trees allowed residents and visitors access to the beach by foot, cart, and wagon. The public streets, marked with the names of families who lived there, were created from those old lanes.

Despite the bridge and eventually a highway, Grand Isle remained an isolated community. It was not incorporated as a town until 1959. Residents needing governmental services needed to travel all the way to Gretna. Self-reliance was and remains a trait necessary to life on Grand Isle.

Although there are street numbers on Grand Isle houses, there are no mailboxes. The house numbers are for emergency responders not mail delivery. Residents pick up their mail at the post office located, ominously, at the intersection of **Louisiana Highway 1** and **Cemetery Lane**. That street is so named because of the old burial ground to which it leads. There, generations of islanders are at rest, with some of their tombs carved with inscriptions in French. One of the tombs contains the remains of Louis Chighizola, the son of the flamboyant Grand Isle resident, pirate, and henchman of Jean and Pierre Lafitte, also named Louis Chighizola, a sailor of fortune from Genoa, Italy. Chighizola *père* had the nickname *"Nez Coupé,"* "Cut Nose" in English. The legend is that he had lost part of his nose in a sword fight. His descendants still live on Grand Isle, and the family name is perpetuated on **Chighizola Lane.**

Jean Lafitte, legendary privateer, smuggler, pirate, and hero of the Battle of New Orleans, is very much part of the rich history of Grand Isle. Although his headquarters were on Grande Terre, the island across Barataria Pass east of Grand Isle, he had at the height of his operations hundreds of people working for and in association with him. He had storehouses and other caches on Grand Isle. He employed the local people to service his ships and boats, and he most likely bought food and other supplies to outfit his vessels and feed his crews. With all the association with the famous and mysterious Jean Lafitte on Grand Isle, it would be fitting to name a prominent street for him, one would think. But the only prominent street on Grand Isle keeps its generic name, **Louisiana Highway 1.**

There were two brothers who lived on Grand Isle, boat captains who took recreational fishermen out into the Gulf. Hamilton and Hector Landry were well respected for their ability to find fish. They lived in houses on streets one block apart. Because everyone on Grand Isle in the early 1950s knew everyone else, Hamilton's street was called **Landry Lane.** Because Landry was Hector's name, too, his street was known as **Hector Lane.** The names of the streets remain after the brothers have gone.

The name Hector originates in one of the oldest pieces of literature, Homer's *Iliad,* the story of the ten-year war between the Greeks and the city of Troy. The great but tragic hero of the Trojans was Hector, who was killed in battle by the Greeks' great hero, Achilles. In an odd coincidence on Grand Isle, a few blocks west of **Hector Lane** is a street named **Trojan Lane**. There is no connection, however, only coincidence. **Trojan Lane** leads to Grand Isle High School, whose mascot name is the Trojans. Also by coincidence there are **Hector Avenue** and **Hamilton Road** in Terrytown. It is interesting to imagine a connection between those two streets and the Landry brothers of Grand Isle.

Those are not the only Jefferson Parish streets with the same name as the Trojan hero. There is another **Hector Avenue** in Old Metairie, but it was not named for Hector of Troy. Monsignor Bezou wrote that the Metairie **Hector Avenue** was named for someone's dog. Maybe the dog was named for the hero from *The Iliad.*

The biggest annual event on Grand Isle takes place on the last Thursday, Friday, and Saturday in July. Officially founded in 1928, the Grand Isle Tarpon Rodeo is the oldest continuing sport-fishing contest in America. The tarpon, once called the Silver King, was the principal attraction, but with dozens of species of fish now eligible and thousands of entrants trying to catch them, the tarpon's popularity competes with amberjack, king mackerel, redfish, speckled trout, and many others. Near the end of **Louisiana Highway 1** at the east end of Grand Isle, a permanent pavilion houses the display, trophies, vendors' booths, and presentation stage. You can reach the pavilion by turning from the highway onto **Tarpon Rodeo Road.**

When Grand Isle was incorporated in 1959, the land in Jefferson Parish west of the Caminada Pass bridge was included as part of the new town. This area is the site of the tragic community of Chênière Caminada, destroyed by the hurricane of 1893. Before that storm, the community was more populous than Grand Isle itself. Today it is merely an adjunct to the island. This area is the southernmost part of Jefferson Parish. It includes the beach, marsh, and sandbars known as Elmer's Island. Once the property of the Elmer Family, it is now owned by the state of Louisiana and open to the public for fishing and beach recreation. To get there, drivers travel at their own risk. So says the sign on the gate. Four-wheel-drive vehicles are best for going to Elmer's Island, open from dawn to dusk. The road is called, no surprise, **Elmer's Island Road,** and it is the southernmost street in the parish, ending at the beach on the Gulf of Mexico.

From the **Metairie-Hammond Highway** in Bucktown, Jefferson Parish's most northeastern street, and **Mesa Verde Street** in Kenner, its most northwestern street, to **Elmer's Island Road,** its southernmost roadway, there are hundreds of streets. Some have interesting names; some have interesting history; some have both; some have neither. But all make up an interesting and varied place to live.

Elmer's Island Road is the end. There are no streets in Jefferson Parish beyond, only the Gulf of Mexico. Anyone who has not been informed and entertained by the stories of Jefferson Parish streets thus far can get cheered up by driving along **Joy Street** in River Ridge and **Happy Street** in Marrero.

Index